The Cairo Incident

Memoir of a Life-Changing Experience

by
Norman Lang

The Cairo Incident

FIRST SUNBURY PRESS EDITION
Printed in the United States of America
August 2011

ISBN 978-1-934597-50-7

Published by:
Sunbury Press
Camp Hill, PA
www.sunburypress.com

Camp Hill, Pennsylvania   USA

This one is for Ilona

To Walter
with best wishes,

Norm Lang

FOREWORD

In March of 1965 I was living in Cairo at a time when Egypt and other Arab countries considered themselves to be at war with Israel. The Suez conflict was still fresh in the minds of many people and it was common knowledge that the regime of President Gamal Abdel Nasser – in power since the army deposed the Western-oriented King Farouk in 1952 – was using German experts to construct surface-to-surface rocket sites in the Sahara desert, the target being Israel. Since the war of 1948, which created the state of Israel in what had been Palestine, there was nothing but tension in the Middle East, of which Cairo was the capital. We all knew this. But we were young, invincible, all there for reasons of our own, most of which had nothing to do with international politics. In my case I was teaching mathematics at a former British school called Victory School in the suburb of Heliopolis to the north of Cairo. We all thought life was pretty good, living like kings on our Western salaries, doing what came naturally. None of us really cared about East, West, the Cold War, or the fact that we were living in a nest of spies.

I say "none of us" cared about these things. There might have been a couple of exceptions to that, not only amongst the journalists in my group of friends.

In February 1965 there was an event that soon dominated the news media in the Middle East and certainly in Cairo. A German national called Wolfgang Lotz – a supposed ex-Nazi, of which there were a good number in Egypt at the time – and his wife, Waltraud, were arrested by the much-feared, Gestapo-trained secret police and accused of spying for Israel. Not only accused. At the time of his arrest, which to say the least is an intimidating procedure in the circumstances, Lotz confessed his guilt when they found a radio transmitter concealed in a set of bathroom scales in his luxury villa near the pyramids of Giza.

It was the talk of the city. In the expatriate community, at the foreign embassies, at the school where I taught, in the cafes where men smoked hookas at night, in the street, and maybe even in the warrens of the tenement buildings where women and children lived their unseen lives, there was talk and speculation. This man was in trouble. His wife, too. Germans working for the Jews? Goodbye life.

We talked and speculated for three weeks. My friends were journalists, lecturers at the American University, colleagues at the school where I worked, embassy officials, and others. Things were going on in Cairo. A spy ring had been penetrated and Lotz was only the tip of the iceberg. It was all very interesting – from the safety of course of not being involved in any way.

At that time I had lived in Paris during the Organisation Armée Secrète (OAS) bombings in the early sixties. Straight out of college with a degree in theoretical physics, I was taking a year off before graduate school, teaching English conversation. That year an average of fourteen plastic bombs went off each day in Paris. From what they read in news reports, my parents thought I was living in a war zone. I recall being in the vicinity of one or two bombs that year, not close enough to be in any danger either time.

No such nonsense going on in Cairo. Just an ex-Nazi spying for Israel who managed to get himself arrested, which as I mentioned could be an intimidating process if you're part of it.

I learned this firsthand in the early morning of March 15, when I was wakened before dawn in my apartment in central Cairo and escorted down to the street outside. There I caught a glimpse of the cars lined up along the blocked-off street before I was pushed into one of them, blindfolded, and driven off.

In speaking of my friends I mentioned "a couple of exceptions" who might not have been politically neutral. One of these was British, a compatriot of mine, and the other German, both of whom got out of the country at a time when other people were doing the same. When I say, "other people" I mean other spies, getting out soon after, or in some cases shortly before Wolfgang Lotz was arrested.

For a number of reasons, some personal, I have let a lot of time go by before writing this memoir. But I can truthfully say that the events of that shortened academic year in Cairo have never been too far from my mind. It was in fact a life-changing experience.

Before I start I wish to say that this memoir was completed in draft form in December of 2010. Since then the chapters that tell the story of our lives in Cairo leading up to my arrest have not been adjusted to reflect the momentous events that began in January of 2011. It is pure coincidence that I decided to write the story when I did. A discussion of torture, incarceration, and the hopes and fears resulting from historic changes taking place in the Arab world today is reserved for later chapters.

Norman Lang
February, 2011

CHAPTER ONE

Sunday, Monday. The alarm went off and I was awake. A moment later I knew what day it was.

After six months in Egypt I was well accustomed to the different work schedule at least until it came to Sunday morning. The workweek ended on Thursday which therefore felt like Friday. Then came the real Friday, followed by Saturday, which, though it was a working day for some people, was still Saturday to myself and many expatriates. Then it was Sunday morning and you felt that Monday had come a day early.

For all that I was in a positive mood when I rose that Sunday in late January. The sky was grey and cloudy. It had been that kind of winter. But I saw a little smile in the full-length mirror and knew that the biorhythms were in sync. Vermelle had not stayed over. Her work ethic ordained that she wake in her own apartment, preferably alone, especially on Monday – sorry, Sunday morning. But it had been a good weekend. I switched on the English channel and headed for the john.

On the way I took a quick look around the new apartment. Walking under archways between the rooms I enjoyed the spaciousness and the view from the tall windows. Outside there was Midan el Tahrir, Freedom Square as it had been renamed in 1952. Behind the palm trees sat the Nile Hilton alongside the river. To the right, the Egyptian Museum, pink and inviting, and to the left, the stark Mogama building which housed twenty thousand bureaucrats. Beyond that the Cairo Tower was just visible in the mists of Gezira Island.

Until the beginning of that year I had lived in the northern suburb of Heliopolis. Now I had my own place in the center of the city, and like most foreigners, I had a servant to do housework. I had no idea where Fatima lived, but she had been recommended by a friend and I had no problem giving her a key so that she could come and go as she pleased. It was a different life in Cairo, but it grew on you.

While scraping my face in the bathroom, I recalled a scene from a couple of nights earlier in a place called

1

Maxim's Bar on Kasr el Nil (Nile Street, renamed from
Suleiman Pasha). Drinking at the bar there was a thick-
necked, very pale-skinned individual with an accent I knew
well. A Glasgow native, who worked on an oil rig in the
Gulf, he was skeptical when I said hello and introduced
myself. When I asked him which part of Glasgow he was
from, his answer was, "You're no from Paisley." I told him
the street where I'd been born and the school I had gone to.
He was not impressed. In retrospect I realized that these
were funny times internationally. He had probably been
warned to beware of friendly-seeming strangers when
ashore. All the same it was a bit of an eye-opener to a
friendly young ex-member of the Glasgow University boxing
team to be called a liar by a native of the city.

In the kitchen I poured boiling water over a couple of
teabags in a mug and headed back to the bedroom.

There are two reasons why I remember that morning.
One was that I would be losing a friend that day – another
compatriot as it happens – but gaining a nice car while he
was on an extended trip to Europe. His name was Martin
MacKay and I would be driving him to the airport that
evening. I was thinking that I would be sorry to see him go
but having the car would solve my traveling problems for a
while, when an item on the radio caught my attention.

While looking in the mirror and tying my tie I heard that
after months of hesitation, President Nasser had invited
the East German President Walter Ulbricht to visit Cairo.
At that time I had a part-time job as a proofreader for *Al
Ahram*, a government run newspaper with an English
language version. Through this I knew that the Soviets had
been pressing Nasser to show solidarity with East Germany
by inviting Ulbricht, a gesture that provoked angry protests
from West Germany and the United States. I heard the
item but thought little of it at the time. Nasser was playing
East against West, as usual, and world leaders were
bickering like teenagers. What was new?

Being in good time that morning I carried my tea to a
window and took a moment to think about some of the
friends I had made in Cairo. Around the corner from my
building there was the Cairo campus of the American
University. I'd met some people there who had lived in the

city for a while and knew it very well. Also a couple of journalists, English and American, who often seemed to know more about what was going on than was ever made public. To the south of Tahrir, behind the Mogama, there was the embassy area and Garden City. That was where I had met Vermelle who worked for the U. S. government. She was a bit of a straight-arrow, but I sensed undercurrents there that were yet to be explored. (I might also mention that acceptable single women were even harder to come by than private cars in Cairo at that time.) The oldest and longest standing resident of my acquaintance was an elderly Englishman we knew as Squadron Leader Hindle-James. He lived in Old Cairo in an apartment that was filled with grinning boys from dawn till dusk. I played chess with him from time to time and he was the one who had recommended my servant, Fatima.

But my closest and in some ways most enigmatic friend in Cairo was Martin MacKay. Of some dubious Scottish lineage – he spoke of Drumnadrochit Castle on Loch Ness as though it were his family home – he worked for a company called Investrade in Europe and possessed a private plane as well as a current model Ford Corsair. Martin was ex-Royal Air Force, about my own age or a bit older, and lived in a rented house in Heliopolis. We were different types but had a lot in common. He was one of those friends that you can know for years and never remember a single conversation you have had with them but who are a part of your life. I looked forward to having the car but would miss his company while he was gone.

And then of course there was Vermelle. It certainly seemed that not too many minutes passed these days before my thoughts returned to her. As the old song says, I was a young man and could play the waiting game when I had to. Which was fine by me. Especially in Cairo, where most of us did not have much to wait for along those lines – unless of course you were a well-heeled young roué like MacKay.

I finished my tea and rinsed the mug. Old habits die hard. Fatima was trying to train me to just leave everything behind me. I checked my briefcase and went down to where I'd parked the car. The date was January 27, 1965.

CHAPTER TWO

When I first visited Martin Mackay at his place in Heliopolis he was lying on a couch eating chocolates with a glass of Scotch and reading James Bond. As often happens when you meet people of similar background, we spoke without formality and I joined him in a glass of Johnny Walker. That was in September of the year before, soon after I arrived in Egypt. A few nights earlier we had met in a sporting club where I was taken by colleagues from the school where I worked. Recognition was by voice. He heard mine and rose from a table where he was sitting with a companion. It was all very friendly, except that the young lady in his company did not seem overjoyed by the intrusion. At the risk of seeming obsessed with the fact, I'll mention again that for every unmarried female in the foreign community in Cairo there were five or six non-spouse-accompanied males, at least three of whom were gay. That still left thin odds, unless of course you were irresistible like MacKay. I told him I was teaching at the Madrasa el Nasr and he gave me his card.

Scotsmen can be con men. They are naturally matter-of-fact, which inspires trust, and often have an innate sense of inferiority, due to their country being overshadowed by England, which gives them a deceptive air of vulnerability. MacKay was a natural. Educated in one of the well known Edinburgh schools, certainly intelligent, but not intellectually intimidating, he attracted people. He was a wiry, dark-haired man of about thirty. Not physically intimidating, but he had the military background and no lack of confidence. Possibly due to seeing my wrinkled brow when he first spoke of it, he hadn't said too much about his family background. To be honest I took the story about highland ancestry as a line for the benefit of foreigners (or for young ladies like the one whose steady smile did nothing to make me feel welcome that evening). But he was definitely Scottish and oozed money from whatever source. At that time it did not occur to me that he might be anything other than he seemed.

4

When I visited him that evening I was greeted by his servant, a balding man named Joseph and a tail-wagging young Alsatian, which looked at me hopefully. From his couch, MacKay spoke sharply to the dog and shook his head at its wiggly, puppy-dog demeanor.

"They're supposed to be watch dogs," he said. "This little bugger loves everybody."

"He's still a pup," I said. "I was raised with dogs and he knows that."

He waved a finger at the bottle as I took a seat. "Do you think they know that?" I nodded. "Like when you take them to the vet?"

"Sure they do. They sense if you're relaxed. If they smell adrenalin it makes them nervous."

His smile was thoughtful. "Maybe that was Julie's problem the other night. She smelt adrenalin."

We laughed. Come to think of it, I was probably more relaxed with a strange dog than with a strange woman.

In the months that followed we palled around on a regular basis. He sometimes talked about his job and other interests but not too much. He was generous when it came to driving people around, but was not given to throwing out invitations to his house, at least to male friends. He liked Americans. When we went to places like the sporting clubs, which attracted foreigners and rich Egyptians, he seemed at home in that community. One exception was Vermelle. For whatever reason she was not one of his favorites.

I met Vermelle at a function organized by the American Embassy in the Semiramis Hotel. My invitation came from an English journalist called Hugh Mooney, who worked for one of the London papers, and an American called Jim Picton, who was correspondent for an American news agency. At the journalistic gathering much of the talk was of the Vietnam War. Why exactly were we there, doing what and how, defending the world from what exactly, were the kinds of questions in the air. In those days I paid little attention to such matters. Like most young people I was concerned with what affected me directly. But that didn't mean I couldn't be provoked by someone with whom I disagreed. A case in point was a gentleman whose position and rank are lost in the mists of time. I remember scant hair, blue eyes turning pale, and hands with thick fingers that literally quivered with emotion when I challenged what he said. His premise was that there is no such thing as an undemocratic war. War had to be approved by the United States Congress which was elected by the people of the United States and if anyone were to be blamed it should be them. I said I knew nothing about what happened in America, but when it came to war I had never heard of one in which the people had any say whatsoever. Even real wars, like World War II were no exception. I challenged him to name any war that was either started or terminated by the people.

Perhaps the gentleman was prescient. Perhaps he sensed that the war in question was destined to be unique in history as the first (and last) that would essentially be stopped by the young people of his country.

For my part it was a rare piece of political opinionating. I couldn't really have cared less but I remember a tall, balding gentleman whom I noticed frowning at me for a while before he cut in with smooth British tones and diverted the conversation. Mooney handed me a drink. The six-foot-five Picton was gazing at the ceiling far above our heads and I was addressed by a smiling black woman whom I had noticed listening with wordless but expressive interest.

"You're pressing buttons," she said gently. "The news from Saigon has everyone a little jumpy."

"Who is the gentleman?" I asked. As usual I had no recollection of his name, even though we had been introduced.

"That's Charles Palmer," she said. "Your Consul General." I realized that she was speaking of the Englishman who had intervened.

"I meant the other one."

She smiled. "That's my boss."

I held her eye. She wore a grey dress with a high collar covering her neck and her hair was pinned up in an austere style. "All right," I said. "You don't want to give his name. I'm Norman Lang. My friends call me Norrie."

"Norrie?" She seemed amused.

I transferred the glass of wine from my right hand to my left and offered it to her. At the same time my gaze moved down the bridge of her nose, as though it were a highway, going from the brown eyes to the lips, which had lost all expression under scrutiny, before moving back and very directly to the eyes. "Now you're supposed to tell me yours," I suggested.

There was the slight sound of suction as her lips parted. I realized that we could be in the field of vision of her boss, who was behind me. She took my hand with a very gentle grip, a gesture I resent, especially in females, because it seems to say, You are doing this, not me.

"I'm Vermelle," she said. "Vermelle McCord."

CHAPTER THREE

MacKay's car was parked in one of the side streets between the main drags of Kasr el Nil and Talaat Harb near my building. It was an area with fruit and vegetable carts where I shopped on an almost daily basis. I have never eaten so much fresh produce as I did in Egypt. Meat was in short supply, but between fava beans and seafood from the Mediterranean I did not feel short of protein.

The only car I'd ever owned was an MGTC circa 1947 which I bought in England. It was now parked in the street outside the apartment where I'd stayed in Finchley Gardens in north London. It was a magnificent little machine, a two-seater that you drove almost lying down behind a bonnet like the prow of a ship; pillar box red. Driving to my parents' house in Scotland, I had crossed the snow-covered Pennines, the big diameter wheels pulling me along under the unheated canvas and plastic top when even the commercial trucks had pulled over.

MacKay's car was my first experience with American technology. As I pulled out into the honking madness of Ramses Boulevard I saw glances that were both envious and hostile. In multi-lanes of traffic you drove in a straight line or else, foot ready for the brake and hands on the wheel. In that sense it was like London, but with differences. I saw a bus career across a couple of lanes and swing around a corner. The driver had probably had his first pipe of the day. The inside of the bus was filled to capacity. Extra passengers, mostly younger men and boys, were clinging to the outside. Crossing the lanes they cut off an elderly gentleman on a bicycle, his galabiya hitched above his bare knees and a baker's board loaded with bread balanced on his head. In the traffic noise I did not hear but saw his lusty yell as he wobbled in the honking traffic to avoid the bus and nearly fell. I watched where I was going and before long I was in the rhythm and driving automatically. One is nicely free to think during the undistracted business of driving, or showering, especially driving.

One of the attendees at the embassy function where I first briefly met Vermelle was a very different young lady a couple of years older than myself, whom I shall call Eva. She was Czechoslovakian, from Prague, good looking, intelligent, employed by one of the news agencies. I was not seeing her for the first time that night. We had met a few times in one of the breakfast places and I'll report that she was not only good-looking but attractive in my view. After the embassy party a number of us went to a bar that we called Ali Baba's and I found myself talking to Eva.

"I hear you have a new flat," she said.

"That's right."

"Hugh tells me it's a nice place." She was referring to Hugh Mooney.

"I heard of it through Hindle-James," I said. "It's an older place, I like the atmosphere."

"Hugh says it's huge. Too big for one person."

I told her I had three bedrooms, two large public rooms, a kitchen, bathroom and a hallway that was as big as some apartments. It wasn't fully furnished yet but I had all I needed. The building had a cranky old elevator with an ornate ironwork front that you could see through. Egypt was not yet populated with lawyers who would sue the building if an unwatched child stuck its hand through. My neighbors were quiet middle class families.

She sipped her wine. I had no objection to being the object of her attention. "Can I come and see it?" she asked. "I don't mean right now. Sometime soon."

"What's wrong with right now?" I said.

She agreed and we walked through the busy streets of nighttime Cairo to my building.

Eva had good shoulders and athletic movement. You could see she had been a dancer. We went to one of the windows and I saw her gazing at the lights of Gezira Island in the Nile.

"It's beautiful," she said. "Like l'Île de la Cité."

"You've been to Paris?" I said.

"Oh, yes. I studied there. After Charles University."

"What did you study, Eva?"

"Philosophy. Journalism." Her greenish hazel eyes met mine.

I offered her a drink. She was more interested in seeing one of the bedrooms again. "My place is not so good," she said. "I think I'm going to give it up." I said nothing. You can do a lot of thinking in a second or so. "Have you thought of sharing this place?"

I told her I had not. Not at least until this moment. At that time I had no experience of eastern European women. Then I heard her proposition.

The next day I called Mooney and said, "How about breakfast? There's something I want to talk about."

"How did you make out last night?" he asked.

"That's what I want to talk about."

Mooney was a frequently smiling, thick glasses, baggy trousered Englishman with common sense and intelligence. We met in a place that served eggs and had drinkable tea. I told him that Eva had decided she would like to move in with me. It offended her sense of economy to see only one person in such a nice big place. She had picked out a bedroom and had some basic furniture. She couldn't pay much rent, but it wouldn't cost me anything, would it? I could even get rid of Fatima and she would keep the place tidy. No sex of course. She had a boyfriend back in Belgrade, or wherever. We would live together like brother and sister. It would be nice to have company though, wouldn't it?

Mooney had a couple of questions. Did she really mean no sex, or just not sleeping in the same bed every night? I said so far as I could tell she meant exactly what she said. No sex. Not even playing doctor. Mooney ate some scrambled eggs. He used a bottle of HP sauce, which he had them keep for him. The waiter proudly called it our Horse Power sauce. I saw him thinking and waited with interest.

"I think it's a very fair offer," he said. "When she says not much rent, she means no rent. I would tell her she can move in for free, keep the place neat and tidy, cook for you now and then and you'll fuck the arse off her every night."

I didn't put it quite that way. I took Eva for dinner to one of the places I frequented on Talaat Harb. She arrived smiling and confident, anticipating her new life. After a while, I wondered aloud how it would work, living like man and wife except for one thing. It would be nice to have company, yes. But we were both young adults. Wouldn't that begin to get on our nerves a little bit?

She understood exactly what I meant. I was a young man. Of course I could bring other women to the flat. She wouldn't mind at all.

I suggested gently that perhaps they would.

She was very quiet, she said. She would just stay in her room. She would not have company. She had a fiancé after all.

That was very nice, I said. Maybe he could visit us from time to time.

She began to get the message and a little tear appeared. For whatever reason, I could see that she was really set on moving in. To be honest, I damn near relented. Hell, maybe it could even work. Then I saw her toss down a glass of whisky with a bleak expression. I covered her hand and said maybe we should think carefully before going any further. Just possibly even her fiancé might not understand.

To this day I haven't figured it. Was she as self-centered as it seemed or the world's greatest innocent? I took her in a taxi to the tiny place she had in old Cairo. What would I have done if she had asked me in? I could say I would have kissed her on the cheek and said, Thank you so much, I would really love to, but no. Maybe. She was unusually physically attractive.

But she did not. And things always work out for the best, don't they? I didn't know it then, but my life in that respect was about to change.

CHAPTER FOUR

I taught at the Madrasa el Nasr, Victory School, renamed from the prestigious British school it had once been. It was in Heliopolis, meaning City of the Sun. In ancient times it was a city of religious significance and is now an upscale suburb of Cairo.

In British terms it was a secondary school, meaning for ages of about eleven to seventeen. The students came from all over the Middle East. There were a good number of boarders, some from well-to-do local families and surprisingly enough it was coeducational. Apart from some religious studies, which so far as I could see were not heavily emphasized, instruction was in English, though the full-time teaching staff was mostly Egyptian. There were some wives of Europeans stationed in Cairo who taught part time, and a small number of European students. But so far as I recall, the only native English-speaking full-time staff were an elderly English gentleman who had been there for many years and myself.

When I arrived in August of 1964 I was met at the airport by a science teacher called Mr Touhami. He was a tall, polite man, who like many Egyptians could have been Spanish or Italian, wearing a western style suit like many business people in Cairo. We put my bags in a car that was owned by the school and drove the comparatively short distance to the campus.

During the drive I learned that Mr Touhami had moved to Cairo with his family some years earlier. I was forward enough to ask him how he liked it here and a slight hesitation before answering made me glance at him. "The school is good," he said. "The town is fine. My children are happy. But I don't find a friend."

I knew what he meant. He was not speaking of a mistress or a lover. He was speaking of a friend he could talk to. I found the admission rather touching. It was a common enough condition, but seldom verbalized in our society. I wondered if he had half hoped that I might fit the bill but had quickly seen it was not likely.

The school consisted of stone buildings surrounded by a high wall in an older part of the upscale suburb. There was a parking lot and buses that transported local students to and from the school in a system similar to what I have seen in the United States. The students wore uniforms of navy blue and grey. The boys wore blazers and grey pants and the girls likewise with grey skirts. Apart from the sound of their voices and the predominance of dark hair, we could have been in the school I had attended in Scotland.

As it happens there was some excitement that day over an incident that had taken place the day before. A female servant had seen two boys, one eleven and the other seventeen on the roof together and reported it. Both boys, who were from significant families, had been immediately expelled and were already off the premises. Someone reported this to Mr Touhami who mentioned it to me. I remember wondering what I would have done had I been the witness.

My living quarters were on an upstairs level that contained the boys' dormitories. I had a bathroom and a small electric water heater. The agreement was that I'd have room and board in return for some house-mastering duties which I could relinquish after the first semester if I so chose. My salary was based on what I would have earned in London, which made me quite well off in Egypt. From the window of the room I looked down on a street outside the school. In the days that followed, I became accustomed to the sight of a cart with wobbly wheels that came by at lunchtime every day with a great urn of fuul, the brown bean stew that was a staple of the local diet. Women and children would emerge from nearby dwellings with saucepans that the old Arab would fill, while his donkey stood patiently. I have always been a people-watcher. Unseen at my window, I would examine the faces, bodies, gestures and behavior of this new aspect of humanity.

It was a different world from anything I'd known. But I was young and soon settled in. On weekends I'd take the train to Cairo where I soon started meeting people. Unlike Mr Touhami I was not a married man with children. Also I was of a sociable disposition. The students were respectful. In the classroom they were diligent and seemed appreciative of my ability to explain the mysteries of algebra and science. The main problem I recall was the overpowering stench from the shells of sunflower seeds which they loved to chew and expertly eject from their mouths when the seed had been removed. I did not allow this in my classes. But other teachers did and the shells and their aroma were in all the rooms, filling the nostrils and crunching underfoot. I became friendly with most of the boarders in my charge. I supervised their evening study and some recreational periods and they were curious about life in Europe.

I recall a couple of incidents. One Saturday morning I was doing my rounds, shirtless because of the heat, wearing what we call a vest in Britain, a sleeveless undershirt. In one room there was a table set up and a boy behind it, the sweat glistening on his skin. He was a well-built boy, obviously a weightlifter, whose name I recall but will not mention. Enough to say that he was related to the ruling family of Kuwait. The boys asked me if I would care to arm wrestle with the one who was obviously their champion. He was muscular, but only about fourteen or fifteen and I didn't have much doubt. But I could see they were divided about who would win, so I sat down opposite. After a tussle, his powerful looking arm gave suddenly and from the way the others crowed I could tell he had been boasting. I then had a moment of remorse, though not regret, and said truthfully that I thought he was very strong for his age.

There was another morning I remember. This time they were all sitting on their beds and watching my reaction as someone closed the door of the room and the spokesman, a sixteen-year-old, said they had a question they would like to ask. "It's not a silly question, sir," he said.

I saw the furtive grins on other faces. "Is it going to make me laugh?"

"Do you promise you won't be annoyed?"

"Don't keep me in suspense," I said. "What's your question?"

14

He checked the room as though for last minute moral support before saying, "We have been wondering. Can a vagina resist a penis?"

I did laugh. Then I saw what they were driving at. I told them that to the best of my knowledge it could not. There were no muscles that could tighten the opening. I hoped that was medically accurate.

To be perfectly honest I have forgotten the name of the elderly countryman who was my house-mastering colleague. I'm sure it was not Green but I'm going to call him that because I never saw him dressed in anything except the pale shade of green of an old sports coat he wore. He was of medium height or a little shorter, with greying hair and an air of quiet melancholy without which I cannot picture him. I do not believe I ever saw him smile. His speech indicated London and he told stories of the Luftwaffe bombing – the blitz as we called it – when he was a young man but not in the military because of some physical defect. I learned later from the boys that these were the only reminiscences from his past life that they had ever heard him utter.

During my months living in the school I had remarkably little interaction with Mr Green. He was in charge of younger boys who required more supervision than those in my area. I don't think I am doing him an injustice if I say that I think he resented my appearance on the scene, which had long been his territory, and in fact his world. As for his sexuality I don't think it necessary to say anything except that I'm sure it was entirely sublimated. I have a couple of memories of Mr Green.

There was a boy in one of my classes whose work was deteriorating and with whom I found it hard to communicate. He was a boarder in Mr. Green's area and one day after an incident I brought up his name, speaking carefully. One was always a little careful when speaking to Mr Green. He was doing something at the time and didn't seem to hear. I asked if the boy was having trouble in other classes or just mine. Was there something I should know? I could see that my questioning was not welcome but being born with the set of genes I have I persisted anyway. Which country was he from? Finally Green answered. "He's

Egyptian. That's all I really know about the boy." I asked if he was local, from Cairo in spite of being a boarder. Why I asked that I don't know, but I remember Green's answer, or part of it. He said something about the family not being very communicative and added, with reference to the boy, "He looks desperately unhappy." I felt rebuked. I recalled the sharp-drawn face of the youngster who would never meet my eye and said no more. I was struck by Green's remark. Not because it was a remarkable observation, which it wasn't, but because there was empathy in his words. Sometime later the boy stopped attending the school and I never learned why.

The other memory might seem trivial, but it sticks in my mind. The father of a Czechoslovakian boy visited his son that Christmas and left a couple of bottles of Scotch, one for Mr Green and one for me. I learned of this belatedly after not receiving my gift, a fact which I conveyed to Mr Green. He was not apologetic. He did not mention that my salary was many times his. He just told me he had drunk the Scotch and pointed out, in his words, "You did nothing for the boy." That was true. What he had done I don't know, though it probably wasn't easy for the young foreigner in the Egyptian school. I forgave the old bastard for drinking my Scotch, but never forgot it.

When I pulled into the parking lot that January morning I did not fail to notice a couple of large gentlemen stationed just outside the school gate. They paid no attention to me as I drove in, for which I was somewhat grateful. A week or so earlier a feisty young Libyan boy had been injured in an accident with one of the buses. I believe he sustained a broken leg. As a result the boy was promptly shipped back to Libya, and a couple of days later the large gentlemen appeared. The bus driver had wisely disappeared and was not seen again in the vicinity.

It was a normal day. In one of the classes a couple of boys who had been boarders in my section reminded me that I had promised to take them into Cairo to visit the Museum on the coming Friday. I assured them I had not forgotten. At lunchtime I joined some teachers who were sitting outside, and one of the part-time ladies, a good looking German woman, asked me what I thought of

Nasser's decision to invite Walter Ulbricht. As I recall she was the wife of a diplomat stationed in Cairo

"What is there to think?" I asked.

"They are protesting in Bonn. Also in Washington."

"That's what they do," I said. "Who gives a ..." (I thought of the word 'monkey's ...' then the word, 'tuppeny...') "toss," I said.

Her blue eyes met mine. "I'm sure you know there are ex Nazis living in Egypt. They trained the secret police and there are scientists working in the desert."

"I've heard of that," I said.

"Whose side do you think they're on?"

I began to see her point. In Egypt at the time, the word 'Israel' was a dangerous word to even utter. As I would soon learn, when driving MacKay's car, the attendant filling it with petrol might ask, "Do you love Nasser?" And even I knew better than to give a humorous answer. At the same time I had no inkling that any of this would ever affect me.

Schoolteachers as a breed are accustomed to speaking without interruption. This can be very obvious when you converse with them. But when the headmaster, a heavyset man with graying hair who was in the group that day, decided to offer his opinion on the morning's news he did so without competition.

"Bonn and Washington are in cahoots," he said. "They work together and are not on our side. I want Nasser to tell both of them to go jump in the lake. Our ally is Russia, not America." I was waiting for him to say that it wasn't Britain either, but he left it at that.

Before the end of the break I strolled to the front gate where some of the students liked to hang around eating snacks. "Where's the fuul-seller?" I asked.

One of the boys shrugged. "His cart fell apart. A wheel came off and the donkey kicked it to pieces."

"Oh my God!"

A month or two earlier I had asked the same boy, whose name was Ahmed, to speak to the fuul-seller. He had to fix the wheels of that cart I said before they collapsed on him. Ahmed and the other kids listening were reluctant to comply. I guess they knew the Arab attitude to

17

maintenance. They took the Christian attitude toward God's will but actually acted on it. Now I heard the story of the fuul-seller chasing his urn along the road as it spilled its beans while his panicked donkey demolished the cart.

"What's he going to do?" I asked. "How's he going to live?"

The privileged youngsters smiled and gestured. "Allah will take care of him," one of them said ironically. I remembered the bus careening around a corner that morning. The Mercedes buses in Cairo were a gift from the German government. Every so often one of them would disappear, like the fuul-seller's cart, never to be seen again. When they broke down, that was it. The will of Allah. One could not accuse the faithful of being hypocritical.

CHAPTER FIVE

I had barely walked into my apartment after returning from the school that afternoon when the phone rang. I picked it up and saw my smile in the hallway mirror when her quiet drawl said:

"Hi, babe."

"I just walked in," I said. "You're obviously psychic?"

"Not really. I just know things."

"Sounds like the CIA," I said.

"I missed you."

"Well, that's easily remedied."

"Want to come over tonight? I'm cookin'."

"Tonight? I'm driving Martin to the airport."

"Oh." I heard the change in her voice.

"I'll be back by nine or so. Is that too late?"

"Give me a call. And Norman. Take care."

I knew what she meant. I said I would and we left it at that.

I switched on the radio and freshened up. I was glad she'd called. The cryptic warning reflected her opinion of MacKay. In the bathroom mirror I saw blue eyes looking a mite thoughtful and a mouth that matched their expression. As a general rule whatever you saw in the one was likely to be reflected in the other. I looked at the straight nose between. I tend to notice noses and the nostrils under them. As a child I used to wonder why God had put a nose in the middle of the face. Why not a blow-hole closer to the lungs? In profile I saw a sloping brow, not as dead straight as I would like, but straight enough. I could not complain too much about the face I had been given. And I was glad that the nose-people had won out against the blow-hole faction in the big design committee in the sky.

With an hour to kill I went to the main room. For furniture I had a sea chest that served as a coffee table surrounded by colored cushions on chairs and against the wall. I sat at a small table by the window to write a letter home.

One thing my parents could not complain about was my diligence as a letter writer. In those young days of course I had plenty of time for everything I cared to do. All the same, I was a mite distracted that afternoon.

MacKay and Vermelle had not exactly hit it off when I introduced them a week or so before. I even saw his lips pull back an unintended fraction when he first laid eyes on her, which I'm sure she did not fail to notice. We were in Groppi's tea room on Talaat Harb. It was the first and only time I'd visited the place, which was Vermelle's choice, and MacKay and myself might have been the only male customers. When we walked in I saw his eyes scan the room. He did not pick out Vermelle, who was already there due to the fact that he had been late in picking me up, which already had me a bit on edge because I'm one of those people who likes to be on time. I observed his face again when he realized which table we were heading for. Contrary to my usual tell-all nature, I had not told him she was black.

"Martin MacKay, Miss Vermelle McCord. Scottish Nationalism meets U.S. State Department. Please shake hands."

They did. Smiling now, he sat down and looked at her, his brow wrinkled in the slightly world-weary, sophisticated air he liked to adopt. "Excuse me staring," he said. "You're very good looking for the State Department, Miss McCord."

"Vermelle," she said. "Thank you. They pick us specially."

"Oh, don't be modest. Did you go to Harvard or Yale?"

"Princeton, actually."

"Princeton? Is that Ivy League?"

"For fuck's sake," I said, looking at him.

"I have a friend who went to a place called Colgate," he said. "Have you heard of that?"

"Oh, yes."

"Ivy League?"

She sipped from the coffee she had been served and shook her head. "It's up there, though."

"Up where?" I asked.

"I meant it's also a good school. But actually it's in upstate New York."

"What did your friend study?" I asked MacKay. "Dentistry?"

"I don't know, but he's a photographer," he said. "He's one of our crew."

In the conversation that followed, Vermelle took a special interest in a film MacKay was working on in the desert. It was a documentary or commercial film of some kind, commissioned by his company, which ended up never being made. I recall that he answered her questions with increasing diffidence and then launched into a digression about a night club called Sahara City out by the pyramids and an English snake dancer who worked there. During this a waitress arrived with a pot of tea, pastries and coffee for Vermelle. While she was selecting from the tray MacKay sat back and lit a cigarette.

"Well, I can see you're not much interested in drunken snake dancers," he observed. "So what does the State Department do for excitement when it's in Cairo?"

Vermelle smiled at him. "We date Scotsmen."

I looked at her in surprise. MacKay gave his sophisticated smile and we chatted on without much being said on either side.

Having tea in Groppi's was like having your hair cut in a salon that deals exclusively with rich ladies. You are entitled to be there, your money is as good as theirs, but don't expect to feel at home. It struck me that it might be similar to being black in the United States. When we checked out, MacKay and I fought briefly over the bill before he let me pay.

Vermelle's flat in Garden City was in a building run by the U.S. Embassy. The lobby was protected by an armed guard who looked more of a threat to me than anything I had seen in the streets of Cairo. There was what I can only call stiff conversation in the car as we drove there. I can't really say who was to blame for this. Verbally she might have started it. In manner maybe he did. They just did not take to each other. And I of course am not the world's greatest ambassador. He dropped us off and winked at me as we said goodnight.

21

The flat was a well-appointed one bedroom with a sitting-dining room and kitchen, which was standard issue for a single person she told me. She put on some music from the Beatles and asked me what I'd like to drink. Glancing at her selection, I asked for a Jack Daniels and Coke. It was the first time I had been alone with Vermelle. If her unexpected rejoinder this afternoon presaged more interest than I had hitherto seen, that was all right with me. We settled on either side of a coffee table, I on the couch and she on a chair opposite.

I saw her hair down for the first time as she untied it. She kicked off the pumps and pulled her feet up on the chair. I sipped my drink and she glanced at me over hers.

"Your friend Martin seems uptight," she said.

"It's just his way," I told her.

"Does he have a thing about Americans?"

"It's not that," I said quickly. She was referring to her skin color. "British people tend to be more direct than you guys. More outspoken."

"Why is that?"

"I don't know." I laughed, thinking of something. "I saw an English comic once who was back from America. He was telling his audience that Americans are very polite people. 'That's true!' he said and told them the reason."

"Why is that?"

"Guns," I said.

She smiled faintly. "Has anyone ever told you that you have a way of looking at people?"

I thought about it. "I don't think so. But you might be right."

"If a stranger meets your eye, there's usually a good reason."

"A sexual reason?"

"Usually. Or because you've looked at them. But you just look at people."

"You might be right. What has this got to do with MacKay?"

"He does not just look at people. And he's not outspoken. What exactly is he doing in Cairo?"

"That's a good question. We haven't really talked about it much." I was still trying to catch her meaning. "Are you saying that he was sizing you up?"

"Does he strike you as being independently wealthy?"

"He's got a good job. And he's certainly a ladies man."

"Well, it wasn't that."

She saw that my glass was empty and rose to refill it. In the mirror behind the cabinet I examined her face. She had a tapering jawbone and delicate features, not overly feminine. I figured she was a few years older than me. She was still thinking when she came back. "I wouldn't trust him, Norman."

I felt the smile vanish from my face. "Vermelle, this conversation is beginning to get to me a bit. Do you have a point to make?"

I saw distress in her mouth and eyes. She knew that she was putting down my friend on very short acquaintance and with no good reason. At the same time I could see that she felt strongly about what she was saying. "A private plane and cars and making movies in the desert. Does he ride horses by any chance?"

"I don't think so." I remembered that he knew nothing about dogs. "No. He belongs to a couple of clubs, though."

"And why Egypt? Has he ever said what brings him here?"

I was not entirely unaware of what she was driving at. Egypt was a country that essentially considered itself at war. There was suspicion of foreigners, though at the same time no wish to discourage those with money. We all knew to speak carefully in front of local people. It wasn't only waiters and bartenders who reported to the police. It was doormen, taxi drivers, servants, just about anyone. It was known as the Eye of the City. A network of citizens all alert and watchful of foreigners. I did not know to what extent Vermelle's job had made her especially aware of this. And although I thought she was imagining things when it came to MacKay, I was not totally unaware of why she was asking the questions she was asking. It occurred to me, as a thought I didn't care for, that maybe someone had asked her to do so. I wondered too, though not for long, if she had information that I didn't. The way she spoke did not indicate anything like that.

I looked at my watch and she said she had things to do for the next day. I called a taxi and we agreed to meet for dinner during the week. She came with me to the door. Without the low heels her eyes were about level with my mouth.

"That was an interesting statement you made earlier," I said, and she frowned for a moment before smiling. "Do I take it as a promise of things to come?"

"It just slipped out," she said.

"I like it when things like that slip out."

We kissed. Once, twice.

"I don't want you to go," she said.

The answering device buzzed. I pressed it and the doorman's voice said, "Taxi for Mr Lang."

I kissed her again. "I'll call you."

She nodded and I left.

With these reflections in mind I wrote a letter to my parents. I could always make my life sound pretty interesting if I wanted to. I told them all about the new flat, the arrangement to use MacKay's car while he was in Europe, and Groppi's tea room. I told them that Cairo was a modern city for the Middle East. None of this stuff about women being prohibited from driving or going out in public alone. The women in the street wore shawls for the most part, but not veils. In places like Groppi's they wore European clothes and drove their own cars. In the poorer streets the men and boys wore galabiyas, but shirts and pants and business suits were common. By this time they knew about Vermelle and must have been wondering. I didn't usually talk about my lady friends and couldn't quite say why I did so now. I just wanted to let them know that I was well and happy, because even then I knew that they were about the only people in the world who would worry if I didn't say so. I never was a person who attracted much sympathy or worry even from my closest friends.

CHAPTER SIX

In the street where I'd left the car there were a couple of fruit and vegetable carts that I used regularly. There were vendors in galabiyas and kids on bicycles scurrying around and some women buying items from the carts. When approaching the car I saw a couple of boys watching me and gave them a nod and a smile. They did not respond. What kind of lives did these kids have? I wondered. In Cairo there was more humanity living in a single block than in any other city I had known. Every day I saw people in the streets and had no concept of how they lived. How did they eat? How did they sleep? I had no idea.

MacKay rented a stand-alone single-story house in a middle class neighborhood. Upscale, but not overly flashy, it had a small yard which he hired someone to maintain and a solid gate which was kept locked. For all his sociability he was not a party-giver.

I found him suited up with his bags packed and ready to leave. He gave me a set of keys to the house and asked me to drop by now and then to keep an eye on it. He also gave me the name and address of an English family who would be looking after Wolfy, his dog. I felt sorry for the pup but thought it would be better off than going into kennels, which in any case did not exist in Egypt.

So how long did he plan to be gone?

Martin was vague. Maybe he'd be back by the summer. Maybe not.

Was this business? Pleasure? Both?

Now he was looking at me. Why these questions all of a sudden? I wasn't given to pressing for personal details that were not offered.

We were in good time for getting to the airport. He asked if I wanted a snifter before we left and I agreed.

What after all did I know about MacKay? I could believe his claim to have attended one of the better schools in the Edinburgh area before joining the Royal Air Force. He had told me once that it took the RAF all of fifteen minutes to have complete control of the Suez Canal after Nasser nationalized it in 1956 before American pressure forced them to pull out. In his school days he was not a rugby player or track team person like myself. His talk was of car racing and flying. As for what he was doing now, in Egypt – or Europe for that matter – the vague job description he had offered sounded like the kind of thing ex-military types could get into.

But there was something on his mind tonight. The sudden departure for what seemed to be an indefinite absence was only part of it. We sat down with a glass of Johnny Walker and I was more than usually interested in what he had to say.

We touched on the politics of the day, discussing how Nasser was thumbing his nose at the United States and openly preparing for war with Israel. People raised in Europe knew what war was. Even if they were very young or not yet born when their country was being bombed and threatened with occupation, they know what it means. The funny thing is you still don't believe it will happen again. Those who do see it coming will have no public voice. In 1965 we knew that things were tense in the Middle East but just lived our lives as though nothing would come of it.

"So how are things with you?" he asked after a while. "Still seeing the Black Princess?"

"Oh, yes."

"Have you fucked her yet?"

"No."

When I did not elaborate, he smiled at my reticence. "A treat in store," he predicted. "Do you think she's for real?"

I've often wondered what percentage of the time we are in control of the expression on our face. We can certainly use a smile or a frown to convey emotion, but it can also happen involuntarily. When it does we are sometimes aware of the fact and sometimes not. Not for the first time in recent experience, I felt the smile vanish from my face.

"What do you mean?"

His lips turned inward in a way he had when choosing his words. I saw them move a couple of times as though he were about to speak but thought better of it. "We don't see too many embassy people," he observed finally. "They tend to keep to themselves, don't they?"

"So?"

"So how did you meet her?"

He pulled out cigarettes and offered them. I took one and we both lit up.

"I told you. At an embassy party."

"And you asked her for a date?"

"Not then. I met her again at Ward-Green's place."

MacKay nodded and inhaled. Philip Ward-Green was an Englishman who taught at the American University whom MacKay had met through me. Then he came out with what he had not said earlier. "I think she's trouble."

I was mildly exasperated. Seeing this he made an expression of remorse which was as close as I ever saw him come to an apology. I realized that he was speaking sincerely.

"Was Ward-Green at the embassy?" he asked.

"It was the Semiramis," I corrected. "I don't think so. It was Mooney that invited me."

"So how long before you met her at Ward-Green's?"

"About a week."

"Quite a coincidence," he said.

"Why do you say that?" I asked. But I knew what he meant. To my annoyance I went on to rationalize. "That's how it goes," I said. "You meet someone you don't know from Adam and then you see them all over because now you recognize them."

He laughed. "The Black Bombshell."

"Is that what you have against her? That she's black?"

"No." He shook his head and now it was his face that flattened out.

"Ward-Green knows all kinds of people," I said. "There was a bunch of Americans there."

"But she was on her own? She wasn't with a date?"

"I guess not."

"A week after meeting you she shows up again and gives you the eye. One more question. Had you mentioned me?"

"Had I what?"

"At the embassy party?"

"I haven't a clue! What are you driving at? That she was angling to meet the great MacKay instead of me?"

"Keep the lid on. I'm just trying to get the picture."

27

"What is this picture that everybody's trying to get? As a matter of fact she has mentioned you since. She thinks you're a bit of a fly boy, if you want to know. Why is everybody so suspicious all of a sudden?"

He sighed as though embattled with the same question. His brow wrinkled as though with thoughts a mite too complicated to convey in words. Then he answered with typical bluntness. "Well, I hate to say it, laddie, but I think she's bad news. She's going to report every damn thing you say." He waved a hand to shut me up. "I'm not saying I would throw her out, I probably wouldn't. But if I were you I would not be saying anything to Miss American State Department that you wouldn't write in one of your letters to your mother." That shut me up. I had just been writing home and we all believed that foreign mail was read by the Egyptian police.

If the above exchange sounds like quarreling, it was not the case. It's true that I didn't care for hearing him insinuate against Vermelle any more than I enjoyed hearing her adverse opinion of him. At the same time it did nothing to change the way I felt about either of them. Like most people I make friends or otherwise and after that it doesn't much matter what they do or say, that's how it stays. It was however paradoxical that the two people I cared most about at this time seemed so negative about each other.

Before we left the house, MacKay opened a piece of carry-on luggage and showed me a number of small stones in the palm of his hand, some of which were turquoise in color. They were contraband, he told me. Worth enough to buy a small fleet of cars. He had no intention of declaring them. The Egyptians wouldn't find them and neither would the British when he got to London. If they did he would say they were souvenirs of no value. He seemed very confident that he would get away with smuggling the stones. He gave an address where he could be contacted in England and I drove him to the airport.

The British and European Airways Comets in those days were fast-climbing jets. I didn't wait to see MacKay take off, but I saw another flight shoot into the air like a jet fighter. I then drove back to town, celebrating the fact that I had wheels at least for a while but feeling some disquiet all the same. I had the strangest feeling of being not quite myself and that nothing was quite real. The sights and sounds of Cairo traffic did nothing much to dispel the odd sensation.

CHAPTER SEVEN

At this point maybe a line or two of personal history. Not enough to be boring I hope, just to put things in perspective.

I was born in the town of Paisley, next to Glasgow on the River Clyde. My earliest memory is of opening my eyes one night and seeing a starry sky that was filled with a high-pitched wailing sound and the deep coughing of large, rough-sounding engines just above the rooftops, flying with no lights. The engine noise came from fighter aircraft taking off from nearby Abbotsinch Airport, I was told, going to fight the Germans who wanted to bomb us. The wailing was the sound of air-raid sirens. I was in my father's arms, wrapped in a blanket, as we headed for the air-raid shelters in the nearby Fountain Gardens.

The shelters were semi-underground structures that looked from the outside like great mounds in the grass. They were entered by heavy doors down a flight of brick-laid steps. Inside there was electric light and bench seats along the walls. We were safe from anything except a direct hit, said my father, who was the manager of a plant that built the Hurricane aircraft. Either because of his age, which was late thirties, or business experience, this was his part in the war effort. Naturally I wanted to know what a 'direct hit' was. Whatever the explanation it elicited more questions, to the amusement of people round about, according to my mother. I remember the appearance of the people, mostly women and older men. I remember one large body, who seemed to think it was all a bit of fun, who led the singing that ensued.

Hitler, has only got one ball.
Goering, has two but very small.
Himmler, has something similar
And poor old Goebbels, has no balls, at all.

No, I don't recall the words from that occasion. But I heard the tune and learned them later. And I loved it.

When I grew up I was going to fly these coughing monsters in the sky. In those days war was not something that happened in a distant place and was followed on television. People knew exactly why they were fighting. If they didn't, the Germans would be marching in our streets.

We had no television in those days, but my parents had a large wooden radio to which they listened for the news. One night, after a BBC report about events in Italy, I remember my father saying, "Oh, that's good!" It must have been the feeling with which he said it that makes it stick in my memory. My mother nodded, less impressed, but I could tell that something good had happened.

Germans have blue blood, said the kids I played with in the street. None of us believed that, but we said it anyway because we thought they were a bunch of bastards.

When I was about five I had all the childhood ailments one after the other. Together with my October birth date this meant I was almost a year late in going to school. I remember looking out one day when snow was falling and being heartbroken that I could not go out and play in it. By the start of the next school year I could read and count and argue endlessly, according to family legend. In most schools in the town admission was automatic and based on district, but there was a well-known private school which had an application process and fairly nominal fees. I remember my interview with the headmistress of the primary school of the William B. Barbour Academy, known locally as Paisley Grammar. The school dated back to 1586, when it was founded as a "sang schuil" for choir boys in Paisley Abbey. I proved that I could tie my shoelaces and read a newspaper headline with the word "people" in it, which brought a little shriek of pride from my mother. Then came a question I do not recall, but have heard about since. What did my parents call each other at home? asked the bearded lady. I said they called each other "You". How I talked us out of that one I don't know, but I was accepted into the school.

From early days my school career was not uneventful. I was never a belligerent child. But in the part of town where we lived in those days, when my father was still a junior partner in a wholesale textile business called Glover and

Hardy, I had to run a bit of a gauntlet to walk to school in my conspicuous uniform. No school buses. You took a public bus or walked. I could use North Street or Wallace Street from the wonderfully named Love Street where we lived. I would try and see which street the gang was on and use the other. I was a fast runner for my age, but they weren't all my age. I remember a grey-haired lady at a downstairs window who spoke to me one day and gave me a two shilling piece – a small fortune at the time – just because she had observed me somehow getting to school day after day.

I also remember the German prisoners who worked mending the streets. One day one of them gave me a small steel battleship, beautifully detailed, which I possessed for many years before I finally lost it. I clearly remember that little toy and the big young man with an accented voice who gave it to me under the eyes of an armed guard of British soldiers.

In primary school I did not get into fights; we were not vicious at that age. But if somebody annoyed me enough I would eventually push them, and this happened one day with a boy who was the son of a teacher in the secondary school. He was a brainy kid with a large head and no shrinking personality and there comes a point. When I pushed him he fell against a desk and cut himself just above the eye. He wasn't a baby about it, but the teachers were concerned. I was given "the strap", a slap on the hand with a light leather tawse by one of the ladies. Leaving the school that day I saw his father waiting to take him home as usual. He saw his son with a bandage around his head and I remember his face as he ran to meet him. I ran in the opposite direction.

Primary school lasted till the age of eleven. By then we had a male teacher known as "Pinky" Kerr (after Kerr's Pinks, a popular brand of potatoes). He was a tough-minded little guy whose daughter was in my class. His strap was not a light piece of leather. It was a Lochgelly Extra Heavy which could literally leave your hands black and blue. I was outstandingly his main customer. For the life of me I don't remember what I did to deserve it all, but there was no resentment or animosity. We took it in stride

– as a punishment for boys, not girls – and though none of us noticed it at the time, it was used only on boys who, in the teacher's judgment, would not be negatively affected by it. Later, in secondary school, I remember sweating through many a weekend after being told to report to the powerful gym teacher at 9 a.m. on Monday morning, usually by a lady teacher who did not use "the belt". This went on up to the age of about fifteen or so, when we were old enough to understand more cerebral punishment (or big enough to hit back).

One day towards the end of our last year in primary Pinky Kerr went round the class asking us what we planned to do with our lives after school and possibly university. Most of the kids said they wanted to be doctors, lawyers, scientists, school teachers and the like. When it came to my turn I said I wanted to be a sailor. Pinky rolled his eyes. "You'll probably be a good one," he said. Then, "You mean so you can write about it? Like Moby Dick?" I had never heard of Moby Dick. His eyes looked past me for a moment. "I think you have a feeling for words," he said. In my mind's eye I can still see him sitting there, wearing a light blue suit and necktie at his desk. He told me at the age of eleven that he thought I had a feeling for words and I never forgot it.

In secondary school we tried out for rugby. While we were all keen as mustard at the age of twelve, the gym teacher saw who was viable and we were playing for the school from then on. There was the fifth fifteen for twelve year olds up to the first fifteen for boys of seventeen or so. I played in all of them up to the first fifteen for two years. Broken collarbones were common from tackling. There were several young boys killed in those years playing rugby, none in our school I'm glad to say. Not wearing helmets we did not go in head first. I played the hooker in the center of the scrum, the one who tries to hook the ball back when it is thrown in by the scrum half. I also played wing forward sometimes when we packed three-four-one. Good days. Frozen fields and muddy bath water. Being young.

By this time we lived in a single-family stone house in a better part of town. My father might have hoped that I would take over from him as the sole owner of Glover and Hardy, but I don't think he was too disappointed when I decided to study medicine. In Scotland this meant getting an M.B.Ch.B. – a bachelor of medicine followed by a bachelor of surgery and an internship. I was accepted into the medical faculty at Glasgow University. In our environment this did not imply academic brilliance. A degree with honors in any academic subject, or even an engineering degree was considered more intellectually challenging than medicine – though many bright people entered that field by choice. I had read books on neurology – including an autobiography by an American called Norman Sharpe – and had decided I would be a brain surgeon. I had the hands for it, people told me. And I believed I would be good at it. What is more fascinating than the human brain?

That summer before we started at university I read Einstein's book on special relativity, written in the early nineteen hundreds. Being young and impressionable I was so taken by this that I decided to change my career. I changed from medicine to physics. Being unaware of the lack of communication between university departments, I informed the physics department of this, but not the medical department. I was called to account. I had an encounter with a very irate member of the medical faculty who informed me that I had wasted a year of a man's life by taking the place that he would have been given. I told him I was very sorry. I should mention that in Britain the medical profession is not associated with high earnings the way it is in the United States, but attracts students for other reasons and is selective.

In the first year of honors physics there was a lot of mathematics, which was not my best subject at school (it was my worst). But university math was conceptual, starting with axioms, with less emphasis on computation than high school calculus. I gave it my attention and at the end of the first year was asked if I cared to take a combined honors degree in physics and mathematics for those interested in theoretical physics. I accepted and ended up preferring mathematics to physics.

During my university days I took up bridge and got serious about chess. My mother's relief that I was no longer playing rugby was short-lived when I took up boxing. I was no stranger in the beer bar of the Men's Union. I graduated with friends who were mostly going on to do research in places like Harwell with the Atomic Energy Commission or do a Ph.D. I sent a letter to France and got a one-year position as assistant d'anglais in the Lycée Condorcet in Paris.

The duties of the English assistant were to hold classes in English conversation with the students. By the end of the year I was pretty fluent in French though not aware of having taught anyone very much English. That was my impression, but I heard later that the Oxford man who replaced me the following year was surprised to find the students speaking with a Scottish accent.

In Paris I lived in the colorful Pigalle district next to the old artistic area of Monmartre. Due to a terrorist bombing that year, my parents might have had the impression I was living in the London blitz, but a few plastic bombs per day is a far cry from being targeted by the German Luftwaffe.

In the cafeteria of the lycée I learned the pleasure of having a glass of wine with food, and discovered French bread, Camembert cheese, and garlic. Before long I had a part-time job at the English School of Paris which I remember well, from the Scottish headmistress down to some of the pupils. One day in the dining room the boys were not happy with the salad served at the end of the meal. An American kid whose name I think was Justin complained that it had "bugs all over it." "Eat them," I said. "They're good for you." He held out his knife with a long, green caterpillar looping along it. "What about this, sir?" I took the knife, tapped the caterpillar onto a piece of lettuce, chewed it and washed it down with water (no wine in the English School). I don't know how much the boys remember of the mathematics I taught them, but I'm sure some of them recall the eating of the caterpillar.

During that year I wrote my first unpublished play and had a number of adventures that are not the subject of this memoir. Still not ready for postgraduate work and a life of science, I spent a year in London teaching in a place called

Quintin School in St John's Wood. It was an eventful year in the days when you do so much in a year. I relate one apparently minor incident because of the embarrassment I caused myself. I never forget embarrassment.

One day the poet Stephen Spender visited the school. He asked the question, What is poetry? Guess who answered. In confident and unequivocal terms of course. Spender let me talk. I remember the tolerance, in a man not noted for suffering pomposity, with which he managed not to inflict too much embarrassment on a young schoolteacher. There is however nothing to protect me from my own hindsight. Defining poetry indeed.

By this time, although they never challenged me on it, my long suffering parents were surely beginning to wonder when I would put to use the education I had acquired. Not any time soon, it seemed. One day I wrote to the Egyptian Cultural Attaché, received a response, and by August of 1964 I was in the city of Cairo.

CHAPTER EIGHT

The Friday after Martin MacKay's departure for Europe was a busy day for me. In the morning I honored a promise to a couple of boys who had been in my section of the boarding school. Their names were Mustapha and Ahmed and I had promised them a trip into Cairo to visit the Egyptian Museum. To be frank I'd made the promise in a loose moment when one or other of them had expressed an interest. In the event I felt a little odd taking just the two of them and not a whole group, but they didn't seem embarrassed. They were waiting with their hair brushed wearing colored shirts, not school uniforms, and when I showed up in MacKay's car they jumped into the back seat.

As we drove from the school there was an incident that was typically Egyptian. After turning onto a divided highway, I was surprised to see the fast lane taken by a huge military tank. It didn't take much thought to pull over and give him space, as did all the traffic on the road. The progress of the tank was, to say the least, erratic. A couple of times the treads were on the median of the highway as though the driver were unsteady at the wheel. The boys said it had to be from the base nearby and I learned later that they were right. There was a large military base not far from the school. I was beginning to wonder if the tank planned to commandeer the road all the way into Cairo when it suddenly veered right before turning left and crossing the median, flattening everything in its path, before causing similar havoc on the other side of the highway. Then it revved its engines and raced back the way it had come.

"I'm glad that's over," I said. "I'm glad he wasn't after us."

"If he were after us," said Ahmed, a normally quiet boy whose father was a government official in Upper Egypt, "it is everybody else who would be in danger." This caused a sharp guffaw from Mustapha, a pert boy who seemed to find endless humor in life. The Egyptian army was well equipped they let me know, but not the best trained in the world. The same driver or his brother would probably be flying a MiG-15 this afternoon. They were also parked near Heliopolis, I was told, supposedly hidden from our enemies.

After that the drive into Cairo was the same as any other day, with multiple lanes of honking traffic dodging this way and that. I got on the road, put my foot down and kept my wits about me. The closest I can come to describing the experience is driving in New York City. Twenty or thirty minutes later we were in the streets behind my building. A youngster in a galabiya walked in front of us, signaling for the car to slow down. The boys told me I should have driven at him and made him jump. I saw them look with interest at the back-street life which might have been not much more familiar to them than it was to me.

I parked the car and they insisted on seeing the entrance to my building. I was aware that none of their other teachers, even the headmaster, would be able to afford the rent of a place like this. I promised that we'd go up to my apartment later and have snacks. Walking across the square I pointed out the Hilton, a symbol of America, and the forbidding Mogama building of the Stalin era. We stopped to examine the gesturing figure of Ismail on his pedestal, after whom the square had originally been named. A hundred years earlier the land where we stood had been marshland, flooded every summer by the waters of the Nile. It was the ruler Ismail who had the vision to have the area drained, but he never got much credit for it because he ran the country into debt. The fact that he made Cairo into a major international city is largely forgotten. "He should have started a war," I said, with no disagreement from my young companions.

Even from the outside, the pink structure of the museum seemed designed to draw us in. With Western and Soviet influence present around the square its colorful façade was like a symbol of Egypt. I said something of the sort, tweaking their nationalistic pride. We paid the fee and hired the obligatory guide. The boys had money but I

38

sloughed it off, knowing it was as nominal to them as it was to me.

To be honest I am not a great museum person. By no means disinterested in our historical past, I am just not much given to spending a lot of time walking around inside a building to learn about it, especially as part of a guided tour. But I must say that it turned out to be a fascinating afternoon.

I think the guide had Scottish ancestry. Once we'd paid for the privilege of being there, he didn't care if we stood and listened to his perorations or made our own way around the labyrinthine passages, which is what we did. We chose the passages, and being surrounded by the art and artifacts of people living two and three thousand years before the birth of Christ was a unique experience. I began to feel something. Call it the oneness of humanity, spanning time as well as distance, given the minuteness of the human race in space and time.

To begin with one saw the essential universality of all religions, whether theistic or monotheistic, ancient or modern. The difference between the theologians of ancient Heliopolis, or two thousand years before that, or an American televangelist today, is less than the difference between two people living on the same street. The motivation is identical and even many of the fables are the same.

We all stopped and stared at a clay miniature of a woman. About twelve inches long, it showed her sitting in a back-leaning posture. The artfully rounded face was totally without features except for two expressive slits for eyes, both closed. The hair was indicated by small mounds around the face and behind the head, which was supported on a long neck leading to a narrow torso with down-turning stumps of arms expressive of a readiness to clasp and cuddle. No breasts. But massive hips and thighs surrounding a small vulva and distinct slit of a vagina in the naked figure. The effectiveness of the small sculpture from five or six thousand years ago was breathtaking. Who says that impressionism is a modern invention? The expression on the face with neither mouth, nose, nor open eyes was unmistakably tender, warm and loving, the massive undercarriage inviting equally to newborn child or grown man. We all looked at it without words for several minutes.

"That is my sister," said Mustapha.

Ahmed chuckled and pointed back to a wooden statue entitled *Sheik el Beled*. We had all noticed that one too, with its powerful, haunted face and bright, staring eyes made of inlaid colored stones. The painted wood was cracked and marred but the perfection of the features and the timeless expression in the face and eyes was undiminished. No modern art school could have produced better.

"That is my father," said Ahmed.

Mustapha shook his head. "I don't think so." He dug his companion in the ribs. "He is not handsome enough to be your father."

"Shut-up!" said Ahmed.

We walked past ancient mummies that gazed back unseeingly. Now we were eye-to-eye with people who had lived before the pyramids and again there was no space or time between us. Wherever it came from, the light was a mixture of blue and yellow which some would call a shade of blue and others would call green. We stood face to face with Tutankhamen.

There were no loud voices in this area. Even the schoolchildren were stilled in the spooky silence. I saw some of them cling to each other as their wide eyes roamed around.

The boys were fascinated by the incredibly ugly head of Akhenaten, father of the boy king. The protruding nose, lips and chin behind the elongated head were indeed not prepossessing. Akhenaten was the son of Amenophis III who had horrified the priests of the day by marrying a commoner, a Nubian woman named Tiyi. When Tiyi produced a son the priests declared him illegitimate, only to find themselves in turn declared irrelevant by this ancient forerunner of Henry VIII of England. One of the most touching and imposing statues was of the Pharaoh Amenophis, seated with his controversial wife, both almost naked except for head gear and with expressions of peaceful rapture on their faces. His hands were on his knees, but her right arm was around his waist.

As serenely beautiful as her husband Akhenaten was threatening and ugly, the bust of Queen Nefertiti took the eye. Between them they continued to challenge the priests throughout his reign and could be said to have invented monotheism, a trend that was soon reversed by their son Tutankhamen, who came to the throne as a child. We gazed at the boy king's famous sarcophagus, authorized by the reinstated priests, and at the golden, ever youthful figure of Isis, the Universal Mother who guards his shrine. I glanced at the faces of the boys and smiled when Ahmed said, "That is my sister." Looking at the buttocks of the youthful, naked figure and the posture of the legs, I could see a modern child standing there. For once Mustapha had no comment.

When we crossed the square and went up to my apartment, I had snacks for what I thought was a pleasant little lunch. But what intrigued the boys was the smell of a curry I'd been cooking. I informed them that curry houses had become very popular in England. Introduced by immigrants from our colonies they were now more numerous than Chinese restaurants and fish and chip shops combined. Being handy in the kitchen I had devised a recipe by trial and error and had a pretty good beef and mushroom curry in a large pot, with rice and baladi bread to go with it. The boys admired the treats I'd bought but had to taste the curry which I heated and served with mango chutney. The spiciness was no problem for the young Egyptians. Mustapha ate three helpings and almost nothing else. Ahmed was more polite.

Egyptian television at the time was pretty basic. I hadn't bothered to get a set, but I had a short wave radio that got channels from Europe and I remember a discussion we had that was started by something we heard on the BBC. I suppose it must have come during a lull in the conversation. A famous actor-director had once turned down a female actor, who later became his wife, as being too old for a part in one of his productions. Their subsequent marriage was troubled. The wife, who was also a well-known movie actress, had mental problems. Years

41

later, shortly before they divorced, he turned her down again for a part for the same reason. We all heard this and I added my comment. "What a jerk." My sympathies were with the woman.

It was young Ahmed, a serious and attractive boy, who picked up on this. "Do you think so?" he asked. "Does he have to favor his wife over other women?"

I said I thought he did, especially when she was unhappy at the time and needed his support.

"But for his art? You don't think that should be the most important?"

"Not if he loved her."

"I agree with Sir," Mustapha said. "If he loved her that is more important than a movie."

I do not claim to recall the exact words spoken during this exchange. But Ahmed said something along the lines of, "So what is love? To give a person everything they want?"

"If it's so important," I said. "He should have known. Then she got sick and he kicked her out."

"So you believe a person should favor the one he knows over other people? What is the word for that?"

"Nepotism."

"We know all about that in Egypt."

"We know all about it everywhere," I said.

"So you think it's right."

"I guess not. But I still think he was a hard-line son-of-a-bitch and I bet it was a crummy movie anyway. Have you even heard of it?"

Whatever you think of my pedagogical delivery I recall the conversation because it touches on a subject that has always been of interest to me. As usual it was Mustapha who got the last word. "I didn't know you were so romantic, Sir," he said, bringing smiles to all our faces.

It was a pleasant start to a memorable day. As we left the building for the drive back to the school I noticed that our doorman was more solicitous than usual, greeting us with his best smile and warm good wishes. I remember wondering what he would say in his report to the police.

CHAPTER NINE

The boys were not the only ones interested in the curry. Later that evening I parked the car and took Vermelle up to the apartment for a drink before going out to eat and she got the scent of it as soon as we walked in. The hot spicing was a new thing to her. I saw her brow wrinkle and her eyes intensify as it settled on her tongue.

"Interesting," she said. "Can I have some water, please?" I gave her a glass of Perrier to go with the sherry she had poured. "Hot, but good. Very good."

She was looking especially good herself tonight. Her hair was done in a different style and she was wearing a colored blouse and dark slacks that showed her lines. Don't hold me to it, but although I think jeans were considered a tad casual in Cairo at the time, slacks were okay. I described the museum trip and the comments of the boys including the discussion that followed it.

"I think I agree with both of them. Especially Mustapha." She smiled.

"It's the old story," I said. "They think they're going to grow up and tell their women what to do."

"You think they won't? In Egypt?"

"I'd be very much surprised."

She fished in the pot and picked out a piece of mushroom. I watched the movement of her lips and tongue as she savored it. She caught my eyes on her. "That's an interesting question from such a young man," she said. "What is love?" I nodded in agreement. "But are you really such a softie?" she asked. I'm sure I smiled. "Would you consider your wife's feelings before a film you were making?"

"Wouldn't you?"

"I suppose it depends how much you love a person."

"Exactly."

I saw the corner of her mouth lift slightly. You and Mustapha, I thought. "But hold on," she said. "His wife is also an actress, probably as famous as he is. Shouldn't she know better than to put him in that position?"

"Which only shows how much it meant to her."

"But they are famous lovers. And she is very beautiful, but unstable."

"She tried to bear his children and couldn't."

"Which means he should put her before everything?"

"Yes."

She used a napkin. For a moment her eyes were elsewhere as she dabbed curry from her lips. Then she walked around the kitchen bench that was between us. "You are so nice tonight I think I have to kiss you. Or is this your way of trying to impress me?"

"Both."

We kissed. She initiated it and I responded. Then she came again and I was there. Then again. "Aren't we going out for dinner?" I mumbled. Her lips were there again. Did she know what she was doing? Or did she think we were just kissing in the kitchen? I picked her up. Her arms came around my neck as I walked us out into the hallway. Her eyes were closed, but not her lips. My new Beatles album was on the turntable. I went there and managed to press a switch. Followed by the voice of Paul McCartney I took us to the bedroom and put her on the bed.

First the platform sandals that she wore. Then the pants and underwear, no stockings. Her eyes were still closed but not her lips. I saw the shy tongue appear again like a tiny animal between them. Then I saw her legs. Blink! Eyes closed, legs open, kicking feebly on the covers.

Shirt, shoes, pants, boxer shorts. White socks like an American.

"*Sont les mots qui vont tres bien ensemble,*" I whispered.

Belly, breasts, narrow waist flaring to the hips.

"*Tres bien ensemble.*"

"What's that?"

"Very good together."

"I need you," she said.

It was only later that I realized that she, too, was quoting from the song.

They were still serving dinner at a place on Talaat Harb that we called Ali Baba's when we walked in late that night. During the walk, she took my arm and hugged it close. I ordered the jumbo prawns and she did the same on my recommendation. "These things are big," I promised. "Longer than lobster tails and nearly as thick. The taste is great." The crowd I knew went there a lot and I was hoping to see some of them on this night of nights. As though on cue a couple of familiar faces drifted in soon after us.

Philip Ward-Green was a graduate of Oxford University. Of medium height, sparely built, with a sharp-drawn face that looked as though he were glad to be in out of the cold, he acknowledged our presence with a wave. In fact it was still cool outside in the Cairo spring but not as cold as Philip looked as his blue eyes flicked around. Although he made no bones about being gay, I had never seen him with a likely partner, which was somewhat puzzling. Passive sexually if in no other way, he could surely have found whatever he was looking for in Cairo. He was with his flat mate, Jon Mentakis, a Greek national with a sense of humor almost as wry as the Englishman's. He was likewise unaccompanied and I wondered, not for the first time, if they were in fact an item but chose not to advertise the fact, which was of course entirely their business.

Hugh Mooney and Jim Picton ambled in. A physically ill-assorted pair, often in each other's company but both straight, they joined the group at the bar and somebody bought beers. Stella lager, nothing extravagant. The barman didn't mind. He knew the foreigners would continue to order rounds and leave him a tip for listening to and reporting their conversation.

Remembering one of MacKay's questions I asked Vermelle how she came to know Ward-Green and Mentakis. She said she didn't really, but a girlfriend at the American University had invited her to their party where we met and talked for the first time. I clearly remembered chatting to the staidly dressed black woman who, somewhat to my surprise, kept responding to my observations. Her smiling eyes were on me now as though she, too, were remembering. During this we heard Ward-Green's voice saying, "For God's sake, sit down," as he almost pushed the six-foot-five Picton onto a bar stool and we shared a smile.

The food arrived with an Italian wine I'd ordered. Feeling very contented with life, I saw Vermelle catch my expression when she raised her eyes and my smile wavered. All right, I thought. So you caught me thinking about you. Then I saw her expression change and asked, "What's wrong?"

She used a napkin to dab her lips. "I think they're off," she whispered.

"The prawns?"

She nodded. "They don't taste right."

I snapped my fingers for the waiter. "The lady's prawns are slightly off," I said. "It can happen. Please take them back and replace them, if you will." He looked uncertain, but did so.

I refilled her glass. "Drink up," I said. "The night's a pup."

"Is that Irish?"

"Yes."

We clinked glasses and smiled. I saw the thoughtful look on her face and waited.

"It had been so long," she said. "For me."

"Really?"

"I've been here two years."

I took that to mean two years of celibacy. "Haven't you been home?"

"Only briefly. I went to Luxor last summer."

"That's what I'm thinking of doing," I said. "I get four hundred in sterling at the end of the school year. I'm thinking of going down the Nile."

The waiter came back. "The prawns are fresh," he said. "They came from Alexandria this morning. They cannot possibly be off."

I saw her momentary look of shock. This was Cairo, not New York. The customer was right if he or she happened to be right. "Let me taste them," I asked gently.

I cut a piece of the succulent sea food, chewed it and nodded to her. "It's good," I said. "It's better than good, darling, it's delicious. I think it's the garlic and Egyptian butter that you taste."

Give credit to the customer. She not only agreed, she admitted it. "I'm sorry," she said to the waiter. "It was an unfamiliar spice."

46

He was the happiest man in the world. He loved her more than if she had eaten the meal and said it was the best thing she had ever tasted. I ordered another bottle of wine.

After that memorable night, I was often in the company of Vermelle. We met with friends at the bar, where news and stories were often exchanged. One night we joined them at the bar and met a representative of the American organization CARE, an affable and unashamedly gay man called Gary. He had a truly horrifying story of something that had happened in the city. CARE had delivered a shipment of frozen chickens to be distributed in Egypt. At a store in Cairo, a woman who had been lined up all day saw that the supply was going to run out before she reached the counter and tried to push forward. She had been killed, I assume by accident, in the angry struggle. I had often looked at people in the street and wondered about their lives. This woman had lost hers because she wanted a chicken to cook for her family that night. The story made a deep impression on us.

One night there was a group of Germans, eating and drinking and having a good time. One of them spoke to me in a friendly way, congratulating me for being in the company of one of the few members of the opposite sex present in the room if not in the city. I took no offense at that, or when he added that he could tell we'd had a good time that night already. I was still smiling when he said, "Did you take pictures? Black and white of course."

To give him credit I felt it kind of slipped out after a lot of beer. He was a man not much older than myself and certainly not one of the ex-Nazis who had settled in Egypt after World War II. I would guess that they were probably some of the engineers and scientists working on Nasser's missile program in the desert. I was never a person easily provoked with words. Certainly not to the point of responding with anything other than words. What got to me was a flash of insight into the life that lay ahead for a racially mixed couple and their children. This was not to imply that I foresaw ever being in that position, but in an egocentric world, it reminded me that we never know how another person feels until we have stood in their shoes. I can clearly recall the big, blond young man, who saw quickly that his joke was not funny and tried to be apologetic.

As a foretaste of what was just around the corner in our lives, I will add that I have no picture of the other Germans in the group but feel sure that they did not include either Wolfgang Lotz or his wife, Waltraud.

The next memory comes from the last week of February. Although not much of a diary-keeper and with no head for dates or even order of events unless it's obvious, I can verify approximately when this happened. I was in the apartment of Philip Ward-Green and Jon Mentakis and we were planning to go out for a drink. I was on their balcony, looking at the sky over Cairo and in a philosophical mood when Philip joined me, wincing at the sting of after-shave on his face. Jon could be heard in the bathroom singing, "I feel shitty," to the tune of a song from West Side Story with his own twist on the lyrics. I surprised Philip when I asked him what he thought about personal relationships. Surely the phenomenon of sex was a mystery even to whatever masters of the universe created us? All right, there was the matter of reproduction, which might explain the basic algorithm. But surely all the ramifications that had developed were unpredicted even by them. The absurdity of obsessive love, for example. Knowing his orientation, I asked bluntly if he had ever been in love himself. His pale blue eyes seemed lost in the landscape for a moment, before he refocused and nodded. "It's absolute hell," he said, when I went on looking at him. Then he asked me if I'd heard about the arrests.

That week I had not yet been in the offices of *Al Ahram* which was one of my sources of local news. I had not heard that the Gestapo-trained secret police were arresting not only a number of ex-Gestapo in Cairo, but prominent Egyptians known to them. Philip and Jon had no details, just the fact that something was going on. I was interested enough but had pretty well forgotten about it by the time I dropped them at Ali Baba's and went to pick up Vermelle.

48

Whatever we talked about, the subject of the arrests did not arise. I recall only that I was in an abstract mood that night, which soon changed when we entered the bar.

The moment he saw us Jim Picton rose from his stool and came our way. Of course it was hard to miss the man as he came looming across the room, but it was the way he glanced at Vermelle before speaking that told me there was something special on his mind. Picton represented a television news network in the United States. He and Hugh Mooney, who represented one of the London papers, often had information before it was on the street. As was typical of Jim, he wasted no time in coming to the point.

"I guess you've heard the news," he said, speaking to both of us. I think Vermelle nodded but volunteered nothing. "They've been arresting people by the dozen," he said. "Mostly German nationals but locals, too. Giza, Zamalek, Heliopolis, all high flyers."

"Heliopolis," I said, thinking of the school. "What's going on?"

"We thought at first it might be due to Ulbricht's visit. Just to piss off the West Germans and the CIA. But why the locals?" He looked at Vermelle.

She shook her head. "We know the same as you. No details."

Hugh Mooney joined the conversation. "It's in the international news," he said. "I don't know about the States or Israel. It seems to be the Justice Department as well as state police."

"What does that mean?" I asked.

"It could mean they foresee a trial," Picton said, "if they've really got the goods on somebody."

"Like what?" I kept asking.

"That's what we're trying to figure out, old son," Mooney said.

They tossed it around a while longer. Departments that did not always work together seemed to be cooperating in a series of raids. German nationals and some high level military and government officials were being pulled in and questioned. Being pulled in by the secret police in Cairo was no small thing. It meant the possibility of torture, execution, or disappearing for life. What seemed to intrigue the journalists – and my not very talkative companion – was the fact that it was all so public. If the Egyptians were going to the world press it implied they had something up their sleeve. The word espionage was mentioned.

The night air was pleasant and she took my arm as we walked back to my apartment. As we passed where I'd parked the car, I saw that the banks of windows above the street were mostly dark. It was after midnight. I thought of the dead woman who had wanted a chicken to feed to her family. It was either the Thursday or Friday of that week, not the Saturday, for she was coming up.

The building had a night watchman. Normally you never saw him, but on this occasion he appeared like something in a Fellini film.

"You Miss Vermelle?"

"Yes," I said.

"You must call Mr Frank. An American gentleman was here. Very important he say."

"Thank you," she said. "Thank you. I have to call," she said to me.

I gave the guy a twenty piaster piece. "Who's Mr Frank?" I asked as we went up in the half open elevator.

"My boss."

We found a note under my door. I gave her space and made coffee in the kitchen while she used the telephone. Her face was tense when she came into the kitchen. "They're sending a car," she said. "We're on daylight."

"Meaning?"

"We work around the clock till it's over."

"What is it?" I asked, not concealing my disappointment.

She hesitated, and then told me. It would soon be all over town. "One of the Germans they arrested has admitted to spying for Israel."

CHAPTER TEN

The German born Israeli citizen Wolfgang Lotz was arrested in Cairo on February 22, 1965. It was a few days later when I heard of it in Ali Baba's. By the end of the week the arrests were international news, though Egyptian government announcements were brief and cryptic. Initial reports said only that a number of German nationals, including Lotz and his wife, were being questioned by the authorities.

In the weeks that followed, my information came from several sources. From people like Mooney and Picton I heard what was being said in the international press. At the school I learned what was being said on Egyptian television and in local newspapers and in the offices of *Al Ahram* I saw what was being distributed to the Arab world. When not at the embassy Vermelle spent a lot of time in my apartment and became friendly with my servant, Fatima, from whom we learned what was being said on the street.

Lotz and his wife were arrested in their villa in the exclusive suburb of Giza. He was a horse owner and they were well known members of the Gezira Sporting Club. Rumored to be an ex-member of Hitler's SS, he and his wife were big entertainers of the upper crust in Cairo. They were known for the lavish parties they gave and their generosity to government officials. He had been in Cairo since 1961.

As for the circumstances of the arrest there were some known facts and a good deal of speculation. According to what I read and heard, members of the Justice Department and the Egyptian State Security Investigations Service were waiting for Lotz and his wife when they returned to their villa that evening. Under questioning he confessed to spying and they found a radio transmitter concealed in a set of bathroom scales together with encryption sheets and other incriminating items. Lotz and his wife were being held in one of Cairo's dreaded prisons where they were isolated from outside information and interrogated daily. Other arrests followed.

At that time it was an open secret that Egypt was preparing for war with Israel. At facilities in the Sahara desert, German scientists and engineers were working on surface-to-surface missile systems that would be aimed at Israeli military installations. Russian experts were training Egyptian pilots in the use of MiG-15 fighter jets, which were stationed and concealed on secret military bases around the country. As a supposed ex-Nazi with high ranking friends in government and military circles, Lotz was well placed to infiltrate these projects and gather information which he allegedly transmitted to Tel Aviv.

Most of these facts were known to people who followed the news and to nightly pipe-smokers in the cafes of the city. Lotz was a spy. This was not doubted by locals or expatriates alike. What was less clear was how he had been uncovered. One theory was that the Secret Police knew there had to be spying activity and had simply arrested a large number of likely suspects hoping to sweat something out of somebody. This view was popular in the street and with some international editors who liked to connect the arrests to Walter Ulbricht's visit. But in later years, Lotz claimed that the police had already searched his villa and found the scales prior to his arrest, which would be consistent with the transmissions having been noticed. The famous spy Eli Cohen had been arrested in Damascus the year before and was executed in January of 1965. It has been claimed that Cohen's transmissions were detected and traced using Russian technology.

Whatever the truth of the matter, it was the talk of Cairo. A Jewish spy had been caught and would meet his just deserts. Political capital would certainly be made. West Germany and its allies, the United States and Israel, would be seen as co-conspirators against Egypt. At the time, the CIA and the Israeli Mossad were silent on the subject.

Paradoxically, in a sense, my personal life was pleasant and rewarding in those weeks. I had a companion who came by and was in my arms almost as much as she was in my thoughts. As always, we had no idea what was just around the corner.

CHAPTER ELEVEN

The Japanese Cultural Attaché in Cairo at that time was a gentleman called Yutaka Wada. While I was still boarding in the school he contacted the administration saying he was interested in English language conversation lessons and they referred him to me. Yutaka turned out to be a young man not much older than myself. He showed up at the school in a chauffeur-driven Mercedes and offered me a night on the town at his expense during which my only duty was to converse with him and for which he would pay me by the hour at whatever rate I considered fair. I said, "Fine, let's go and have a beer."

The first night I took him to Ali Baba's where we met some people and ate the prawns, which he enjoyed. Back at the school his chauffeur had a record of the hours spent and asked me how much I wanted. I said, "Listen, this is not work for me. You don't owe me anything and we can do it any time you like." In subsequent weeks we visited clubs in Cairo, eating and drinking and talking colloquial English. He was a married man with an understanding wife who didn't mind staying home while he had his English lessons. So far as I could tell he had no interest in the ladies in the places we visited. We had some interesting conversations and he gave me the occasional bottle of Scotch, which was no small thing and much appreciated in Egypt.

It was after the arrests and the news about Lotz when we went to a club in Cairo and witnessed a brawl between some rowdy foreigners and Egyptian staff attempting to control them. Yutaka, who was a good-sized person and probably no stranger to the martial arts, seemed much amused as we watched from our table while fists flew (no other weapons, I'm glad to say). While the live band blared note for note precisely replicated Beatles music, he told me of the wartime myth in Japan that Americans have larger penises than Japanese men. This was not true, he assured me, but it was curious how such rumors could take hold and persist. We discussed the psychology of racially

53

oriented rumors. Given that they are invariably pejorative, did that mean that Japanese people equate a large penis with a small brain? The brawling had subsided and the harassed bouncers were trying to maintain peace amongst the drunken visitors, who were still being served alcohol, when I heard an accent I knew well and spoke to one of them. "What's the idea?" I asked. "Why come to a place where people are trying to enjoy themselves and start a brawl?" He looked at me as though I did not understand the meaning of a night's entertainment. When I repeated my question – Why start a fight? – his answer was, "Just to see what they would do." As we spoke, he did not seem like a belligerent person.

I also learned how the ruckus had started. A stocky gentleman who had been listening to our conversation pointed to a very tall, but lanky young man in military uniform who was now nursing what promised to be a very painful black eye. "He was telling everybody what to do. I said, 'Well, you're bigger than me so I'd better do what you say.' The stupid idiot didnae know I was kidding, so I gave him one down low and that's what started it."

When it came to the subject of the arrests Yutaka was reticent at first. The Middle East and Israel were not of great interest in Tokyo. He did however have a couple of comments.

Wolfgang Lotz was not a leader of the spy ring, he asserted. He was obviously an amateur being used by Israeli intelligence. He probably did acquire some useful information by taking insane risks, but now that he was out of the picture the network was still very much in place. The Israeli Mossad would have one, at most two, katsas (elite case officers) in Egypt. At this time they would either be deep underground or out of the country, probably the latter. They would not be throwing champagne parties with people who were under routine surveillance.

Did it occur to me, even for one passing moment, that someone I knew well, who was not given to hosting parties, happened to be out of the country at the time? The honest truth is I don't recall.

Like most people I followed the news and talked about Lotz. We pitied the poor bastard, but that was about it.

Most people agreed with Yutaka's analysis, but who really cared? When it came to world affairs I was like most young people: interested in what concerned me directly and not much else. The back and forth between Israel and Egypt and their spy games with each other were not in that category. Quite interesting to read about, but nothing in the world to do with me.

CHAPTER TWELVE

I do not recall who suggested the visit to the hammam (the baths) or how it was arranged. I have stated before that there are things I do not recall in exact detail. I hope this is not taken as a sign of evasion. In writing a memoir, though concerned with facts, it is often tempting to invent where one feels that one can do so without distortion. If you are capturing the true feeling of a situation, perhaps it is legitimate to invent a little for the sake of readability and dramatic effect. As a novelist writing a memoir for the first time, I feel this at every turn and have sworn to avoid the urge, but there are certain small exceptions. In cases where I recall the feeling of a conversation if not the exact words spoken, I allow myself to offer dialogue which would probably not follow the actual transcript if it existed, but which gives the true shape and meaning of what transpired. If an oblong is recognizable as a straight-sided figure and an oval shape is an ellipse or a kind of circle, I feel that the reconstruction of dialogue is justified, even if no one can possibly remember the actual words spoken.

However it happened Phillip, Jon and Gary of CARE, plus myself, made our way to the Bulak district one night and visited the baths. In Cairo the hammam is an institution where natives and foreigners, all male, enter a facility of cement floors and darkened rooms where hot water is everywhere and naked bodies of all ages walk around disporting themselves for one purpose or another. There are older married men who are there to wash and others whose purpose is to have sex on mats which lie in the shadows or in small private rooms with paying foreigners depending on opportunity. After some of the descriptions I'd heard about the goings on in such places there was no way I wouldn't go there to see for myself.

Rather than drive in MacKay's car we took a taxi to the shady Bulak area. We were now in a place of earthen streets where men sat in the shadows smoking pipes while unseen women looked after their young children. The bath house was a great steamy place inhabited by denizens and

occasional celebrities, including a well-known Hollywood
actor whose visits were notorious.

Being wealthy foreigners, we hired rooms in which our
clothes were left in baskets and there were surfaces for
entertaining visitors. They could hardly be called dressing
rooms since one emerged from them stark naked, but so
far as I know, none of them was used for any other
purpose that night. We were supplied with towels for use
after washing, and when we sallied forth, I saw that Jon
Mentakis had a body covered in black hair which matched
his permanently shadowed jaw.

In the center of the main room there was a fountain
where older men were unselfconsciously washing
themselves. I remember reaching for a piece of what I
thought was communal soap, only to have a bather cover it
with his hand and look at me resentfully. I apologized
profusely.

In an area close to shadowed walls, where mats and
some hardly visible figures could be seen, there was a hot
tub the size of a small swimming pool. It reminded me of
the bath in which we used to wash off the mud after
playing rugby at school, but larger and with colored tiles. It
seemed to be a popular resting place and my companions
headed that way while I, as is my wont, explored the
territory. In a side room I saw a swimming pool with a
single occupant. A very large fat person with a huge
balding head was wallowing somewhat aimlessly in the
middle. Against one wall, on what seemed like tiered
benches for spectators at a swimming competition, there
were at least a dozen small, naked figures gazing at me
with mild curiosity. I gazed back, wondering what was
going on. I later learned that the urchins were allowed free
entry out of the night cold, but I received no explanation of
the Farouk-like figure in the center of the pool.

Back in the central area I joined my friends in the hot
tub. And I don't know if my presence made it an untypical
night, but so far as I observed none of them did anything
but enjoy the warm water. The bathers in this part of the
room were mostly in their twenties or younger. I recall one
boy, in his early teens, who was descending one of the

ladders into the pool but stopped halfway, touching his
half erect penis, eyes rolling.

"That kid's drugged out of his mind," I said to Mentakis.

"Yes." He nodded, smiling.

The boy was well put together. He did not look
physically deprived in any way. Seeing my eye on him, he
came into the water and was quickly by my side. I spoke to
him, trying English and French. He said nothing but held
my eye. I was about to ask Mentakis to interpret, when a
couple of the older young men spoke to the boy, causing
him to snap back in an angry voice which I would describe
as broken but only just.

"What's going on?" I asked Mentakis. "Why are they
trying to push the kid aside?"

He shrugged. "They think you want something
different."

I was genuinely surprised. "Why don't you explain?" I
said to Jon. "Tell them I'm just here for fun – I mean, out of
curiosity. Tell them to leave the kid alone."

His dark eyes fixed on mine. "Do you want this boy?"

"What? No, of course not. Why won't you tell him?"

I remember Ward-Green's face, watching and listening.
And Gary of CARE, also missing nothing. Under the
opaque water, I felt a hand on my thigh.

I gripped his wrist. Then I put my clenched fist under
his nose and smiled. The boy's eyes shot fire. I could see
that I had done the wrong thing.

He climbed out of the pool. I clearly remember his clean
form on the ladder, lips muttering.

"What's he saying?" I asked.

"He is saying things about your ancestors," Mentakis
told me.

"Tell him I didn't mean to offend him," I pleaded. "I'm
not here for sex. But if I were, as a matter of fact, it would
be him I'd pick and not one of the others. Can you explain
that without offending him?"

Jon shook his head. "I would need my classical Arabic
for that."

There is an end piece to the story which I could omit but
won't. On our way back to the dressing rooms, Mentakis,
the only one in the group who spoke fluent Arabic, told me

that they were talking about me and admiring my physique in the bath house. All right, I was more flattered than annoyed. Then we were confronted by a little man of about sixty. Wrapped up for the night air in a heavy sports coat with a wooly cap on his head, he stood in front of us, showed his gummy grin and pointed to my chest.

"Me fuck you," he said.

I looked at Mentakis. "Use your classical Arabic," I said.

CHAPTER THIRTEEN

When I returned to the apartment that evening I was disappointed to find that Vermelle had left. There was a note saying that she had to go into the office early the next day and wanted to catch up on some sleep. There was a P.S. saying that a Hans Goslich had been calling.

Goslich? I could not at first place the name. Then I remembered meeting a German who worked with MacKay. He was one of the film crew. I wondered what he wanted.

As for MacKay I had not heard from him since he left. I had a poste restante for him in London but had not used it. I wondered what he was up to. At least he hadn't been arrested at the airport – so far as I knew – with the stones he was smuggling.

At a loose end in her absence I poured a glass of Scotch and walked around sipping it. It's a habit of mine to go home and replay unusual events over and over in my mind, either celebrating some small triumph or the opposite. The scene at the baths was in the latter category. I still had an image of the boy who caught my eye on him and was disgusted when I failed to follow through. I felt that I had inadvertently demeaned his manhood in some way. The world is full of differences from one culture to another. But even in an unfamiliar setting I should have been quicker to understand, especially after the attempted intercession of the older men. This was certainly one that was going to live in my box of memories.

I was pacing and thinking when the telephone rang. From my window I could see the lights and minarets of Cairo around Tahrir and Gezira Island beyond. I went to the hallway and picked up the receiver.

"Hallo?"

There seemed to be a pause before I heard, "Norman! It's Hans Goslich. How are you doing?"

I had completely forgotten about her message. The voice was not the one I had hoped to hear. Then it clicked. "Hallo, Hans. I'm fine, how are you?"

"I'm okay. Been pretty busy lately. How's the new flat?"

"Oh, I love it. Living like a pharaoh. Have you heard from Martin?"

He cleared his throat. "Yes, and actually I have a favor to ask. I also have to be in Europe for a while. At least until the summer. And I don't want to keep on my flat for it's not so great, but I've got a couple of things I need to store. I was wondering if you could throw them in a cupboard for me till I get back."

"Do you mean furniture?"

"Oh, no. Just some suitcases and boxes of stuff. I thought maybe you could stick them somewhere where they wouldn't be in your way."

I was beginning to form a picture of Goslich. A round-faced, pale-skinned man with a way of standing in a casual attitude, always low key, quietly intelligent. Given that I had the use of Martin's car while he was gone I felt that I could hardly refuse the request of his friend.

"Sure," I said. "You're not talking about a roomful of stuff, right?"

"Oh, no. Just a couple of suitcases and one box. Maybe two boxes."

"Okay, Hans, that sounds fine. When do you want me to come and pick them up?" I after all was the one with the car.

"That's great. Thanks a lot Norman." He pronounced my name with the accent on the second syllable. "Actually, I'm leaving in a bit of a rush. Can you come over tomorrow night?"

I genuinely didn't mind. He was an amiable enough character and it was a small request. It did occur to me that we could dump his stuff in Mackay's house in Heliopolis, to which I had the keys. But that would mean leaving it as temptation to servants for a period of months. He gave me his address and I agreed to see him the next evening.

I then resisted the temptation to call Vermelle. I just wanted to hear her voice, but she was probably asleep by now. My news could wait. Instead I sat down to write a letter home.

Whatever my parents thought of me as a wandering son, I was always a diligent correspondent. In the days before email, we sat down and wrote letters. As often happened, the act of doing so triggered memories.

My mother's maiden name was Govan and her family owned a bakery chain in Paisley. One of the retail stores in Well Street had a bakery behind it where my uncles and their helpers worked, making bread and morning rolls and delicious Scotch pies, as well as fancy little cakes and pastries. My favorite were the Scotch pies. Made of water pastry, filled with juicy minced mutton, they were especially delectable when still warm from the oven. During the war my mother served in the front shop some days and I would be around the bakery, watching them work and getting the occasional treat. I remember one day I had a hot, juicy pie and dropped it on the concrete between the bakery and the shop. One of my aunts told me that the devil had kissed it, but she had the wrong guy if she thought I wasn't going to pick it up and eat it. I'm told I always had a sense of humor, but there were limits to it when I was young. I remember one day there was a fighter plane flying low overhead with its rough, unmuffled engine. My uncles came out of the bake house in their white aprons, looking up and saying, "That must be one that Louis Lang built," referring to my father's wartime job. I was not amused. I reported this to both my parents and was scarcely mollified when assured that they were only kidding.

Looking out at central Cairo from my window and wondering what news to send home, I had that feeling that would come over me sometimes that nothing was quite real. The universe, our life in it. What sense did it make? (Meaningful or not I can hardly bring myself to kill an insect, with its one little life – unless of course it gets into my house and bugs me.)

What did it mean that I had told my parents about Vermelle? In retrospect I realize that certain feelings I had were maybe deeper than I knew. Thinking of her brought another memory.

I was in my grandmother's flat above the store on Well Street when one of my mother's sisters called us to the window. In those wartime days before commercial television, before I had even been in a cinema, I had never seen a black person. I knew they existed and might have seen pictures, but this was the first time I had seen one in the flesh. He was dressed in an open raincoat that went almost to his ankles, because it was summertime and we were experiencing what we called a heat wave. As we watched he took a white handkerchief from his pocket and mopped his brow, as he seemed to almost stagger down Well Street in the humid eighty-degree heat. I remember wondering why he was wearing an overcoat and recall the comment of one of my mother's younger sisters.

"You'd think he'd be used to it."

"Why?" I asked. At that age this was my favorite word.

"Because where he comes from it's always hot."

"That's why he hates it," they tell me I declared.

As I wrote the letter I found that she was on my mind. I also wondered what my parents would make of seeing a female friend mentioned not once, but several times and tried to imagine their reaction to the fact that she was not white. I suppose I mentioned that an Israeli spy had been arrested in Cairo but that was far from being uppermost in my thoughts.

CHAPTER FOURTEEN

Hans Goslich lived in Zamalek, a popular neighborhood with expatriates due to its Western atmosphere. His apartment had a roof from which we gazed over the river at the picturesque architecture of central and Islamic Cairo. I could see my apartment building and the domes and spires of the Mosque of Mohammad Ali in the Citadel, lit up in ghostly beauty. Looking for something to say to a comparative stranger, I mentioned my recent visit to the museum and worked in Vermelle's name, vaguely curious to see if MacKay had mentioned her. It didn't seem to ring a bell.

"What do you think of this Lotz character?" I asked. "Is he really a spy or are they just using him for propaganda?"

Goslich did not seem overly interested. "I met the guy a couple of times," he said. "He's a loudmouth. Quite a good horse rider. Sexy wife."

"Is he really ex-SS, or whatever they say?"

He gestured. "I don't know. Lotz is not a Jewish name. But he acts like a Jew."

"They say he was transmitting to Tel Aviv," I said, repeating a government statement. "They say they found a radio transmitter in his bathroom."

"Then he is dead. Jew or not."

I tended to agree.

Goslich had two suitcases and a couple of boxes. We put them in the trunk of the car and I asked him what he was doing with his bits and pieces of furniture. "Nothing much. Do you want them?"

I picked a lamp I could use and some other small things. "You're leaving quite a bit behind."

"It makes the landlady happy."

I asked him if he wanted to store some things at MacKay's place but he said it wasn't worth the trouble.

Goslich offered to come with me to help carry the stuff from the street up to my apartment. I said it was not necessary. He offered to buy me a beer at a local place. I said not to worry and wished him a good trip. We shook hands and I left him standing outside his apartment building, waving to me as I drove off.

Vermelle had no direct comment when she heard about it. By now I knew how to interpret that steady look and lack of comment. It meant she didn't like what she had heard. I was half amused and mildly irked. I knew that one had to watch one's Ps and Qs when living in Cairo and didn't need a lecture on it. But I was innocent of any kind of wrongdoing and was not the type to jump at shadows. In other words I had the grand confidence of a person raised in a free society where justice rules. I was not going to spend my life looking over my shoulder for imaginary threats.

We were in her apartment and I could smell a chicken in the oven. She had poured a couple of shots of a good single malt and I was looking forward to the evening. I saw her looking at my face.

"I know what that little smile means," she said.

"What does it mean?"

"It means you know what I'm thinking and think you know better."

She took the chicken from the oven and began to baste it. I hovered around, smiling. I noted that she had the prominent butt of many black women, though her features were European. I noted her hands, which were long-fingered and capable.

At this point let me try to describe Vermelle a little more. She was not a great beauty in the usual sense, whatever that is. One of the many puzzles to me in life is why some people are easy on the eye and others are not. There is certainly some truth to the statement that beauty is in the eye of the beholder. We judge on things other than physical appearance and you can get used to a face. But there is also a puzzling universality of opinion. Children are seldom repulsive. Why is that? And why are some people prettier or handsomer or just better looking than others? Different cultures have different standards of behavior and morality. One could talk all day on that. But beauty is beauty, wherever you go. Not just of the face, but of the hands, the feet, the neck, the arms, the legs, the set of the hips, you name it. And beauty is not the only word to describe whatever it is. There are just certain combinations of human geometry that draw the eye more than others. In such situations most of us – at least in Western cultures – are conditioned to look away and reveal no interest, especially when most interested or repulsed. I am too, but am sometimes slow to remember the fact, which has caused many glares or quizzical looks back in my direction.

So how do I describe Vermelle? She was not plain, if that makes any sense. But the most unusual thing about her was not the impersonal attraction of sheer beauty. It was something harder to pin down. A kind of serious, intelligent look that gives a feeling of rapport, probably because of the expression in the eyes.

Vermelle, when I looked at her, struck me as a person to whom I could relate. I could see immediately that she shared my values, concerns, not necessarily opinions. Her eyes, whether behind her glasses or not, looked out at the same dilemmas of life that concerned me. A friend of mine once remarked that you need someone you can talk to. The most obvious statement in the world is no less important for being so. It takes one second to know if you like the look of someone. About three words to know if they're intelligent or not. Maybe half a minute to know how much you're going to like them.

I liked Vermelle. Which in my case means that almost no matter what she did or said, I would continue to do so. I forget who it was who gave his son a piece of advice I always remember. He told his son to follow his heart and not be too concerned about what other people think because "those who love you will still do so and those who don't, won't."

I knew that Vermelle instinctively disliked Martin MacKay. She had rational arguments for this, including what could be described as his abrupt departure from Egypt, but that struck me as pretty far-fetched. Now there was the departure of Hans Goslich, also leaving possessions in my care. MacKay had left a lot behind him. An aircraft, a film company, and according to him, a lot of money in a bank. Where had all that come from in the first place? Did I know?

To go with the chicken she had acquired a bottle of Graves from the Bordeaux region more known for its red wine, which she knew to be my favorite. It was a fine little feast and I don't recall much of what we said except for one topic, maybe two.

We talked about the summer. My plan at that time was to take my summer money, which would be paid in sterling, and do some traveling in North Africa, including Egypt. I knew that Vermelle had done that the year before and wondered if we could vacation together during her time off. It surprised me how much she was on my mind. We also talked about Wolfgang Lotz and Martin MacKay and Hans Goslich.

Back in my apartment late that night I went to the cupboard in the spare bedroom and looked at what Goslich had left with me. There was a locked suitcase and two boxes that were lightly taped. I went to the kitchen, got a knife, and slit the tape.

In the first box I found mostly books and gramophone records. There was also a small record player taped up under its plastic cover. The books were in German. I saw names like Einstein, Goethe, Nietzsche, Thomas Mann. Vermelle had asked me if Goslich might be homosexual. I had no opinion on that but flipped open one of the books and saw *Death in Venice* and *Tonio Kroger*. Well, so what? The same kind of stuff could be found in my bedroom.

The second box contained a variety of technical equipment. Feeling guilty for prying into his stuff I opened it carefully, planning to tape it up again later. Suddenly I found myself looking at two small two-way radios. They were of a type that could be used for short range communication only, like people filming in the desert, and were no big deal, except possibly in Egypt. Then I saw recording gear. Tape recorders of the type where the tape was a fine nylon thread. This was state of the art stuff. Now I was thinking. I could certainly understand why Goslich did not wish to go through customs carrying such equipment. How had he acquired it in the first place? More particularly, what did I do now?

Making a movie in the desert? Vermelle could not believe that I wasn't sure what the movie was about. I could only guess that it had something to do with the Suez crisis or the war in Yemen. And what about the private plane? Lotz and his wife were in hot water for driving around and taking pictures. How about aerial shots of missile sites and other installations? Gathering data to be sent to Tel Aviv by some agent – meaning a non-professional being run by an intelligence officer. She was very guarded in everything she said but even I began to get the message.

Then I thought about it a little more. Goslich was working with a film crew in the desert. That could be a perfectly innocent explanation of the equipment. And he was into music. I saw opera and Dixieland jazz in his record albums. What did all this mean except possibly that Mr Goslich was more interested in the arts than his colleague MacKay? The suitcase was locked; I tested its weight but did not break into it. I just closed the cupboard and left everything as it was.

CHAPTER FIFTEEN

In the spring of 1965 we were well aware that Egypt and Israel considered themselves to be at war. You could not enter either country with a passport that was stamped with entry into the other. We all knew that Nasser was attempting to build rocket ranges in the desert and had heard tell of Russian air power concealed on secret bases around the country. We did not know that Israel was planning a pre-emptive strike that would take place two years later, but I don't think many people would have been surprised at the prediction. We knew that there were spies in Cairo, lots of them, but not amongst our personal acquaintances of course. And the secret police were everywhere. It was a tense time. Jews who had been born and raised in Egypt were now mostly in Israel. Other long-established residents, like Jon Mentakis, who had spent most of his life here, were making plans to leave for good. Everyone in the city knew of the arrest of Wolfgang Lotz and many others in his wake. This came close to home in some cases and we talked and speculated as facts accumulated and gossip spread. Lotz was known as a party-giving playboy who had confessed to being a spy for Israel. But contrary to what was being put out by Egypt (and later Israel) he was not considered to be a key player in what was obviously a large scale operation.

During the week that followed my meeting with Goslich I spoke quietly to several people including Mooney and Picton. I learned that the radio telephones were illegal in Egypt and it was dangerous to possess them. The illegal part was news to me, but I am not so instinctively law abiding that I did anything about it except to keep the matter to myself and a small number of friends.

One of the people to whom I said nothing, though I trusted him as an individual, was Yutaka Wada. This in spite of the fact that I was invited to his home that week and the subject arose while we were having dinner.

Until that evening I had never met Yutaka's wife and was frankly curious about her. Not many Western women I knew would be happy to stay at home while their husbands were out visiting clubs that were essentially whore houses in order to improve their language skills. When he invited me to dine with them I was happy to accept.

Not being one who takes automatic note of these things, I recall it as a pleasant apartment situated probably in Garden City near the embassies or maybe Gezira island, but that's a guess. I was driven there in the Mercedes so that I would not be inhibited in taking advantage of the sake wine, which turned out to be a good precaution. After a glass of Scotch during which we talked about life in Britain and Japan, we sat at a formal dining table, just the three of us, his wife and myself on one side - not in adjacent seats - and Yutaka on the other. I believe they had no children. If so they were not present. His wife was a pretty, dark-haired woman whose name was something like Mariko, but that could be a trick of memory.

Earlier that day he had asked if I liked fish. Being from a small country surrounded by the sea I told him it was one of my favorites. He said they had a beautiful fish from Alexandria. I said great, and looked forward to the meal as well as the occasion.

There was an appetizer which was a traditional Japanese dish and was very good. I got all the details at the time but recall only that it came in a brown sauce that was interesting and tasty. I can describe the main course in detail.

The fish must have been a good-sized animal and was served in generous portions of grey flesh, completely raw. I remember the large slice on my plate with what I recall as tiny red veins in it, like blood vessels. Do fish have red blood? I am not a squeamish eater. Octopus, squid, and snails done in garlic butter are amongst my favorites. But the raw fish from the Mediterranean was a challenge. Don't ask me how it tasted. I got it down with green Japanese mustard and lots of the warm sake. Not to imply that I did not enjoy and appreciate the experience, which I recall clearly, including some of the discussion at the table.

I asked a question which I had put to several people. Did they believe that Wolfgang Lotz was really a spy or just a scapegoat of some kind?

Yutaka wiped his mouth before answering. "This is confidential," he said, as though oblivious of the presence of his wife. "They were certainly gathering information, Lotz and his wife. Given how they met and married right away she was certainly an accomplice, but neither one is a Mossad professional."

"Why do you say that?"

He answered as though it were obvious to anyone. "They went around taking pictures of military bases. They drove past a guard onto the rocket site at Suez and then called their influential friends to get them out of it when they were arrested." He shrugged.

"I haven't heard about that."

"Maybe they thought they had connections that would protect them. I don't know."

"Lucky they weren't shot."

"And he was sending regular radio transmissions, which eventually were noticed."

Now I thought for a moment. "They would be noticed," I agreed. "That's how they caught the guy in Syria. And a couple of directional antennas could locate the source." (The "guy in Syria" was Eli Cohen, who had been arrested the year before in Damascus and was executed in January of 1965.)

"That might be exactly what happened," Yutaka said, looking closely at me.

I remember thinking that this Lotz affair was getting more involved the more I heard about it. I was tempted to get Yutaka's spin on the Goslich business, but he was an embassy official and I could not ask him to hear me in confidence. The same was true of Vermelle of course, but I could not keep things from her. I just hoped I could trust her American bosses to be discreet. Whatever I was thinking I still did nothing. I went home that night and looked again at the items in the opened box in my spare room beside a locked suitcase that I did not break open.

Without mentioning Yutaka's name I passed on some of his opinions to Vermelle the next time I saw her. We were in her apartment at the time and although we were saying nothing prejudicial, I asked her if she thought the place might be bugged. She said she didn't think so, but added that they could bug a telephone and a whole apartment all in one these days. They could replace the cradle with one that had a microphone buried in the plastic that would pick up every sound in the room. The only way to find it was to break open the whole instrument.

"Maybe I'll do that when I go home," I said. "And if there's anybody listening to us now, I hope his balls drop off."

I did not destroy my telephone. Nor did I think it likely that the Egyptian police would be so interested in my private conversations. It was a strange feeling though. The thought that an army of sinister people might be watching. I still did nothing about Goslich's possessions. I had no desire either to call the Egyptian police or sneak out at night and throw his things into the Nile.

There was another development in those weeks. Given America's increasing involvement in Vietnam, Jim Picton was given an assignment to Saigon. In order to maintain his Cairo desk he asked Mooney and myself if we would help, and we said sure. We met in Jim's place and he showed us how to tape reports and get them to his news agency while he was gone. I remember listening to what he was sending at the time and trying to imitate his style of delivery. He seemed to prefer my voice to Mooney's – either that or Mooney was reluctant to be so involved because of his own job. I remember thinking that the recording gear was primitive compared with what I had seen in Goslich's possession and might have mentioned the fact. It was agreed that the text of the reports would be put together by Mooney and myself based on what he gathered from his sources and what I saw from my work with Al Ahram. Recompense would be a prawn dinner and as much Scotch as I could drink for me and something similar for Mooney. I was looking forward to doing it. I listened to the punchy American style of news broadcasting and made a practice version in an Americanized Scottish accent. It was fun. It was the kind of thing that could happen in Cairo that would not be likely to come your way in Europe. As I would soon discover this was not the only difference.

That week I started inviting people to my apartment for a dinner party on the Saturday night. I was planning a quiet house-warming. Not a full-scale drinking, dancing party but a more restrained, sit down, eat, drink, and be merry occasion for about a dozen people.

Also in that time frame there was another piece of news. Egyptian television showed a carefully groomed, not beaten up or mutilated Wolfgang Lotz staring sincerely into the camera and telling the German and Egyptian public what a terrible mistake he had made spying for the nasty Israelis against the nice Egyptians. I did not see the broadcast but learned about it the following day in the offices of Al Ahram.

CHAPTER SIXTEEN

From an early age I was no stranger in the kitchen. As a teenager, I would wait till my parents were in bed, then peel a large number of potatoes – Golden Wonders or Kerr's Pinks – fire up the "chip pot" (a large pot full of solidified lard) slice the potatoes into chips and fry up a gigantic batch of them, to be eaten usually with canned peas, which I heated in a pot, the combination seasoned with salt and vinegar. It may not sound like health food, but I recall those midnight meals with pleasure.

For the dinner party I made a large batch of the beef curry on which I had been experimenting. It was served with rice and baladi bread (village bread) which came in a flat round not unlike in appearance the porotas you can get in Indian restaurants in Britain. I also cooked up a spicy dal curry made from yellow lentils and had lots of sweet mango chutney as a condiment. My definition of a feast.

The guests started to arrive at six. I had beer and wine and Vermelle set up a table where she shook martinis James Bond style that tasted to me like straight gin with fat olives in them. The old guard was there: Ward-Green, Mentakis, Picton and Mooney. As well as a house-warming for the new flat, the occasion was a farewell party for Jon, who was leaving for Greece in a few days' time, and a send-off for Jim Picton who was flying to Saigon the following night. Hindle-James was there, grey-haired and cheerful. He seemed very happy to accept a martini. There were two couples who were not part of my usual crowd. Mahmoud Sebah was a teacher at one of the expatriate schools whom I had met a few times and invited after talking to him recently. A quietly fervent man who had fought in the war in Yemen, he was with his wife, a pretty, dark-haired woman called Jehan, who requested orange juice to drink. On the other side of the fence politically there was a couple I had met through Ward-Green. Dan Fried was born in Poland and had escaped the Nazis by way of France, where he was educated before moving to Britain. He was with his wife, a good looking English woman called Jane. The twelfth guest was also different. A French woman called Maria; she had been a nun and was now an academic visiting the American University, as was Fried. An older lady, on the heavy side, very jovial, Maria was introduced by Ward-Green as his companion of the evening and accepted a glass of white wine.

We collected in my main room and milled around the hallway, walking between the arches and looking at the lights of Cairo. My stereo was playing music like the Beatles, Edith Piaf, and Theodore Bikel singing Russian folk songs.

As I may have said, the apartment was not overstuffed with furniture. I have always disliked fancy furniture. It costs money and you're afraid to use it. I had a dining room furnished with a large, well-used but beautiful old table and twelve chairs. For the occasion I had moved all of these into the sparsely furnished main room, the one that had the view of Cairo. The chairs and colored cushions in the room were pushed against the walls with an assortment of small side tables for drinks and snacks. I remember Dan Fried's comment when he viewed it from the arched doorway. "Very inviting," he commented. I agreed and wondered what it reminded him of in his varied past.

Conversation soon got going. Fried and Sebah found each other quickly. The one short, with a large head and soulful brown eyes; the other taller, dark, with darting eyes and a wounded back from his military days. They discussed the war in Yemen, comparing it with the growing American conflict in Vietnam. Jim Picton heard this and joined the pair, towering over them like the Empire State Building.

Hindle-James zeroed in on Maria, the ex-nun. A jolly pair, they took to each other like children of the same age, with no agenda other than what they had in common. I don't know that I can say the same for Hugh Mooney, who seemed to enjoy the words of Dan's wife, Jane. I saw his grin wider than usual and the heavy glasses fairly glistening as they discussed – from what I briefly overheard – what was becoming known as Women's Lib in the

Western world. For better or worse, with all its pros and cons, they seemed to agree that this was something that was on its way. It just had to come.

Preoccupied with his imminent return to Greece, which I saw as a major decision in his life, Jon Mentakis was in a head-to-head with Sebah's wife, Jehan. They were talking about changing times in Egypt. I heard Jon say that he had grown up with many Jewish friends who were now nearly all in Israel. Ward-Green seemed to be in a thoughtful mood tonight. He was losing an old friend and might be contemplating his own future. He asked me if I thought I'd stay another year in Egypt. I said I thought I would. The school was good and I liked the lifestyle in Cairo. We chatted about education. He agreed with me that children were much the same the world over. It was adults that were the problem. During this I heard a hearty laugh that told me Hindle-James and Maria were hitting it off.

I served the curry and dal in large tureens with the rice on platters and the baladi bread, which I had sautéed in oil, in baskets. People sat where they chose along the sides of the table and helped themselves to the food and wine from bottles of red and white that stood around. The host and hostess sat at opposite ends of the table and toasted each other now and then in a way that made me think she was a little more lubricated than usual.

Yemen and Vietnam were subjects of discussion. Picton was concerned that President Johnson was planning to escalate in Vietnam and Sebah did not like what Nasser was doing in Yemen. Both leaders had imagined they could end the conflict with a few air strikes against a primitive enemy. Learning otherwise they were now committed to finishing what they had started, which of course did nothing to dismay the war lovers in either country. It was Mooney who voiced a thought that was shared by most British people I knew. "It may be great strategy to bomb the hell out of people who don't have an air force, but it's not exactly heroic, is it?" In the silence this provoked, we all remembered the presence of Hindle-James.

"We never felt like heroes," the old squadron leader said. "We took off and fought the Jerries in the air. They bombed our cities, then we bombed theirs. It's an ugly business."

For a while we talked about the food.

It was unusual, they all agreed.

Interesting.

Very good, but hot.

Very hot.

How had I made it?

I explained my process of trial and error to imitate the curries I had had in Britain. It was of course typically British to develop a taste for food that is designed to make you sweat in a tropical climate. There was now a curry house in reach of every pub, and they did well when it came to eleven o'clock in London. People would extend the evening by going for a curry and washing it down with red wine.

"I think you missed your vocation," Mooney said. "This food is bloody delicious." I answered a silent toast from Vermelle endorsing this.

While Picton and Sebah were discussing Vietnam, with an interested Dan Fried listening in, some of us touched on the subject of the day – Wolfgang Lotz. What would become of all the people being arrested in his wake, we wondered. The names of some Egyptian military leaders were mentioned. Hadn't they wondered about Lotz? Egyptian men don't think in bed, Mahmoud declared, coming into the conversation. Lotz had a blond wife. He shrugged. They were fools, not spies. The Jews were not fools. I should say that Mahmoud was not averse to drinking wine and was doing so rather steadily by this time.

It was Fried who asked, "You think he's a Jew? I thought he was an ex- Nazi."

Mahmoud laughed scoffingly. "He is a Jew."

Partly to divert the tone of this, I raised the subject of Martin MacKay. For the benefit of those who hadn't met him I gave some background, including the fact that he had left Egypt just before the arrest of Lotz and left his car with me. I also mentioned Goslich, though not the fact that I had possessions of his in another room in the apartment. I was surprised by the reaction.

Those who had known MacKay and met him in my company didn't say much. Mahmoud was immediately outspoken. I was taking a chance, he said. Even the children at the school knew about me driving a big American car belonging to some foreign friend. The students knew I loved them, he said, using the English language in a slightly different way than most Englishmen, but wondered what I was mixed up in. I don't think I have to say that this gave me food for thought.

I recall a brief exchange that I think came also as an attempt to break the quiet tension that was developing between Sebah and Fried. Vermelle asked Jon how he felt about leaving Egypt after being brought up here for most of his life. He said he would miss a lot of things, but not the food. One could get enough of eggplant and beans, he said, a tad wistfully.

"Washed down with orange juice," I added. "Sorry," I said, catching Sebah's wife's eye on me. "Have some more." I lifted a pitcher of orange juice Vermelle had squeezed.

"I think I'll have some wine," she said. "Just half a glass."

I am the slowest eater on the planet. At the age of five or six my mother told me I should chew every bite forty times and I think I still do that. I was still eating curry and breaking bread and sipping wine while other people were patiently sipping wine when I heard something that caused me to raise the subject of love. What is love? I asked the table. The English language is of course deficient on the subject. It equates love to everything from changing diapers to caring for the elderly. I was talking about the kind of love that drives people crazy, men and women.

The question found a surprisingly responsive table. With a range of ages, religions, and sexual orientations represented, the discussion was animated and serious for the most part, with a few exceptions.

"Love is a hard penis." Mentakis.

"We all know it's merry hell." Ward-Green.

"Love is when you start kissing and can't stop." Vermelle. Toasted by myself along the table.

Still eating, I did more listening than talking. They touched on Romeo and Juliet, Adam and Eve, and Thomas Mann. Vermelle said she'd read *Death in Venice* in college and described it as a story of intense longing. That was a kind of love wasn't it, sexual but not consummated? I liked

the description. Longing as distinct from lust. I did not ask
if it were her description or that of her professor at
Princeton. I was totally unprepared for what happened
next.

CHAPTER SEVENTEEN

No one thought anything of it when Vermelle rose and left the table for a few moments. When she returned, she had two pages of lined manuscript- length paper which appeared to be hand written and double-spaced. She handed these to Dan Fried, who had a Ph.D. in psychology, which he taught at London University. He scanned the pages and I saw him smile.

"What is this untitled work? An essay on Love?"

"Why don't you read it to us?" she said.

He did so. Touching his glasses to his nose, peering now and then to decipher the handwriting, he read slowly and carefully in his slightly accented voice and I am able to present the content verbatim.

Love is essentially illicit. The legalized, life-long "love" of the average man is about as interesting as any other property which is common to all of us. Love is not commonplace. In its nature it is violent, one-sided, short-lived and absolute hell to the person involved. "Till death do us part" by mutual agreement, is not love. It is a sound arrangement between two people to live together and raise a family and I am all in favour of it. But it is unsound and unnecessary to confuse this contract with love. The interesting thing about love is that most of us experience it, just once, usually in adolescence. After that we have defences against the recurrence of the condition, uniquely human, which has nothing to do with procreation and is a menace to peaceful existence. Those who fail to develop these defences remain exposed to the extremes of which their nature is capable. They are never content, but always in torment. Because love is often reciprocated, or at least humoured, for a while. Would a blind man prefer his consistent darkness to the occasional gift of sight, emphasizing his condition, which must inevitably return? Actually, he has no choice. Either

he is capable of repeated attacks of love or he is not.
Society frowns on all aspects of love, for obvious
reasons. Poets dwell on it, whether they experience it
or not, because it has no explanation in terms of
biology or evolution, and yet everyone understands
it, or something of it. Why should one person develop
this terrible, useless hunger for another? And how
many adults, from the vast majority who are
immune, would sacrifice their security for a sip of
love? It is little wonder that lovers are persecuted by
all men, not least the object of their love, their self-
destroying love, which they would not relinquish for
anything conceivable by man or god?

Fried finished reading, blew his cheeks and smiled.
"Wow!" from Hugh Mooney. "That kid's got it bad."
"How do you analyze the writer?" Vermelle asked,
addressing Fried and the table in general. "Old, young,
male, female? Sane? Crazy?"
"Definitely young," Fried said. "Probably male. Almost
certainly male. And this is an outpouring. He wrote it all at
once, with some stroking out and corrections. All one
paragraph. Not rewritten or polished. And he makes his
point. Especially at the end."
"Do you think he has been in love?" Vermelle asked.
"Most certainly." There were sounds of agreement from
the table. "Maybe more than once. When he says, 'Those
who fail to develop these defences' – against love – he
originally wrote 'Those of us' and then stroked out the 'of
us'. I think he certainly knows of what he speaks."
"So who with?" she asked. "A girl or another boy?"
"Ah! Good question."
At this point most people had a go at that, with
interesting results. The women at the table assumed it was
a girl, while most of the men thought probably another
boy.
"So how would he grow up? Straight or homosexual?"
"Who can say? Who can really say what the difference
is?"
"That is an interesting question." This came from Maria.
"I have often wondered even what is sex, exactly? I mean,

we see the physical differences. But mentally I'm not sure I know."

"You do not believe that homosexuality is the work of the devil?" Something like this came from Mahmoud, who I'm sure felt outnumbered at the table in terms of culture and religion.

"I do not think that," she said smiling. "Either the male or the female ones, whatever that means."

"So why don't you tell us?" Jane Fried asked. "Who wrote the little outburst – as though we don't know."

To my amazement they all looked at me.

I told them truthfully that I had no recollection of writing the pages. I know I was in secondary school at the time. It was before I went to university. But as for the object of what they all assumed was personal experience, I honestly had no recollection of that either. I had gone to a co-educational school. There were girls and boys and I recalled crushes here and there. But I did not recall what inspired this particular outpouring, if indeed there was a single cause. I just wrote the pages one day and put them in a little black portfolio with other pieces of memorabilia, which I later carried with me on my travels. One night recently I had shown the pages to Vermelle, but it was not my idea that she brought them out this evening.

We were tossing things around again, for a while back on subjects like war and religion, when Hindle-James unexpectedly took the floor.

CHAPTER EIGHTEEN

We had cleared the curry dishes and were eating cheese and salad with crusty bread and red wine when the old squadron leader spoke up. At first I thought he was diverting the discussion from a smoldering debate on what Western leaders called Arab terrorism and what the Arabs call retaliation against state-sanctioned murder – a subject that had arisen between Mahmoud and Dan Fried – but we soon saw that he was raising something that was on his mind.

"I have a moral question," Hindle-James said to the table. "First a religious technicality." He smiled at Maria, the ex-nun and kept us waiting for a moment. "Does God know everything that's going to happen?"

"Ahhh," she said, recognizing an old issue. I was surprised when she turned to me. "You are from Scotland, our fine host. Are you a Presbyterian?"

I knew of course where this was going, or thought I did. "I was born that way," I acknowledged. "And yes, they get into knots between predestination and free will. But I think the logic of it is pretty clear. If God is all-powerful and all-knowing, he can hardly be trapped in time the way we are."

"I think that answers your question, James." In spite of being corrected several times, she called him James. His actual Christian name, which I think was Charles, we never used. "So let's agree on it. Now what is the conundrum with which you wish to tease us?"

"First I have to tell a story, if I may. I'll make it brief. Years ago a friend of mine fell in love with a young woman. She was rather a wild creature, as he was too in those days, and had a young son from a previous husband. At the start of the relationship my friend worried that she wanted to get married, which was not his plan at all. But by the end of the summer, which he described as a great summer for all three of them, he realized he was in love and was surprised to find that marriage was not her plan either. She told him gently that it was time for them to go their separate ways. Still puzzled, he went to her place one

night only to learn from the boy that his mother was out
with another man. She would not be back till later the next
day. My friend found himself alone with the boy, who was
an intelligent youngster. While they talked, my friend
drowned his sorrows with some whisky from a bottle he
had given the woman and ended up doing something which
I know was totally uncharacteristic. We don't need details.
Enough to say that I almost can't believe what he told me.
All of a sudden he put his hands on the boy's face and that
was it."

At this point he paused and sipped some wine. If he was
waiting for a comment it was Dan Fried who obliged. "It
became sexual?"

Hindle-James nodded with a kind of smile. "You could
say that."

"It sounds like lost love to me," Fried said. "For both of
them. The boy was upset because he was losing a father."

"And maybe he loved the boy as much as the woman in
a different way," someone offered from the other end of the
table.

Hindle-James went on. "I can now make the point I've
been coming to. After sleeping on a couch or something my
friend took the boy to breakfast the next morning. Riddled
with guilt he tried to apologize for what had happened. The
boy put up with this for a while before asking the question
I started with. 'Does God know everything that's going to
happen?' My friend mumbled something along the lines
that if He's God, we suppose He must, and the boy asked
his next question. 'Then whose fault is it when it does?'"
Hindle-James glanced around, smiling. "Who cares to
start?" His eye settled on his new friend across the table.
"Does my dear Maria have an answer?"

Her puckered face released a puff of laughter. "What an
ingenious child. Is he a Presbyterian by any chance?"

"Actually, he's ... not that."

"Jewish," said Dan Fried.

"I think it was Christ in the temple," Maria said.

"Come, my dear, don't try to evade the issue. How would
you have answered?"

"I've heard it put this way," she said. "It's like two cars
on a winding mountain road. One is going up and one is

coming down. An observer knows they're going to crash but he did not cause the crash."

"But God did!" I argued. "He put them there!"

"Your friend is the one who did something with the boy," she said to Hindle-James. "No one else. Yes, you can think of questions I can't answer. But no, it does not change the fact. He is the guilty one."

"It didn't end there," Hindle-James went on. "The boy asked what's wrong with homosexuality anyway. What harm does it do? My friend talked about the age difference. Between adults it's controversial. Between children, no big deal. But if one is an adult and one is not, society sees a problem. The boy wanted to know why. What constitutes an adult? Just chronological age? Then my favorite. Imagine this calm question. 'If God doesn't want you touching me, why does he make it so attractive?'"

In the silence that followed this, Mahmoud was the one who laughed. "I think we have all identified your friend," he said. "It is ourself."

Whatever he meant by that was not determined. Jane Fried mentioned Adam and Eve. Whose fault was that after all? But her husband Dan would not accept God's culpability. He talked about winding up a watch which then went on its own. Most of us wouldn't buy that either. Someone asked if Thomas Mann, who had a wife and children whom he loved, would have touched Tadzio had the opportunity arisen. As one who notices such things, I recall again a curious difference that tended to refute Maria's theory about the oneness of the sexes. Most of the men thought probably not and the women weren't so sure. The conversation found its way back to the question about obsessive love. How did Mother Nature come up with that one?

After the cheese and salad, Vermelle produced a chocolate cake she had bought at Groppi's and served it with coffee. I brought out a single malt courtesy of Yutaka, and it was passed around. During this the inevitable happened. The smoldering embers between Mahmoud and Fried flared suddenly.

The Muslim told the Jew that the world was tired of hearing about their "fucking holocaust". The Jew told the

Muslim that they had never intended to kick the Palestinians out of Israel, but he was now very glad they did. Jim Picton changed seats and sat between them, smiling down from one to the other. I made some banal pronouncement about not permitting fisticuffs or head-butting in my apartment. It was soon over. Dan Fried had recollections of being lucky to escape from Europe as a young man. Mahmoud said that was all very well, but why take it out on his people? They both had their resentments, but agreed that it should not be taken personally.

Fried's wife Jane spoke to me in the kitchen. Blond, intelligent, a mature smile on her face, she had no apology for appearing to flirt with Mooney earlier. Nor was it necessary, for we all knew there was nothing to it. "I can't believe it," she said. "I've never seen Dan even remotely aggressive in his life. It's why I married him. I love it," she added.

Which is why we find you irresistible, I thought, but didn't say it.

One more recollection from the party. After a Scotch or two I took Picton and Mooney into the spare bedroom and closed the door behind us. I opened the box and showed them Goslich's technical equipment.

Who knows about this, they asked.

"You guys. Vermelle."

"Give me the stuff," Mooney said. "I'll drive across the bridge tonight and throw it in the river."

"Thanks for the offer. I appreciate that, Hugh."

I meant that sincerely but did not accept. I left the stuff where it was and still did nothing.

Finally we were alone. The next day was Sunday, but Monday was a holiday in the Muslim calendar and we had both decided to take Sunday off. Not being genuine members of the aristocracy, we felt badly about leaving the entire clean-up operation to Fatima, who now also worked for Vermelle, cleaning her apartment once or twice a week.

"Whatever it is about human bodies lying side by side," I told her, "it's one of the things the creators in the sky got right. I'm sure they intended it with procreation in mind but without all the other details. The universe is not the work of some god who sits up there watching everything. I once heard it described as being more like a graduate student experiment – ingenious, but not perfect. Time is nothing. What seems to us like eternity is probably just a couple of hours to them. Maybe it's only milliseconds, like what happens in a computer. We think we're a big deal. But so does a little ant on the floor of your house, with its one little life. It probably feels like a space traveler finding food to take back to its colony. And in the grand scheme of things, whatever that means, who can say differently? It's just as important, or unimportant, as we are."

"Is that right?" she said.

CHAPTER NINETEEN

"You're a light sleeper," she said. "I only have to look at your face and you wake up."

"Keep your eyes off my face," I mumbled. I saw light on the windows. It was later than usual. Memories came back. I thought it had been a good party, which brought a smile to my face.

"Your friend, Hindle-James," she said. "He likes little boys, right?"

"I thought he kind of liked – what's her name? The Swinging Nun."

"She's nice. I liked her."

"I did too."

"Do you think he was telling someone else's story or his own?"

I yawned, thinking about it. "I wondered the same thing. But I spoke to him later and he said something interesting. The woman was no fool. The kid's mother. And the friend was a creative person. An artist of some sort. Creative men don't make devoted husbands. She wanted a devoted father for her kid. That kind of rings true to me, and it's not Hindle-James. He was a soldier."

"That's you," she said. I turned and looked at her. "Now that you mention it, that is exactly you."

My eye was half an inch from hers. It was like looking into the eye of a sea monster. "Do you have a smart-ass little son?" I asked. "Back in America?"

"No and I don't think I ever will," she said. "I have a career."

I think I wondered if she were trying to tell me something,

Despite having eaten enough for three days the night before, I made a bacon and egg breakfast. We ate this with leftover French bread and a pot of English marmalade donated by Hindle-James. Vermelle made coffee and I made tea. Like most people from my neck of the woods, I must have tea in the morning. We talked some more about the future.

At the end of the school year my lump payment would be enough to buy a used car if I chose to do that. I had toyed with the idea of driving down the Nile and possibly spending another year in Egypt. I still planned to do post graduate work someday, but not necessarily in physics. There was so much guesswork in modern physics. I was beginning to prefer the purely human invention of mathematics – which at least in our perception, curiously enough, seemed to have remarkable bearing on the universe in which we live. Even if it was all just a dream.

Could I teach for another year? I thought I could. The school was OK. I did not, however, see it as a lifetime career.

Would I ever go to America? There's a story my parents liked to tell, especially in later years. At an early age, when asked what I wanted to be when I grew up, I once said I wanted to be an American. I later learned that a lot of children admire America, and once they've visited they never want to go home. Electronic gadgets, being treated like VIPs, driven everywhere, never having to walk or take a bus, snacks galore, and endless compliments at every turn. I don't know if it makes great people, but kids love it.

CHAPTER TWENTY

That evening I drove Jim Picton to the airport. He was quietly keyed up about the visit to Saigon and I envied him the adventure. He reminded me that I had promised to work with Hugh the next day to help produce his Cairo report.

It was after midnight by the time I was back and parking MacKay's car in the side streets near my building. As always I looked at the banks of mostly unlighted windows in an area where there would be fruit and vegetable carts during the day, and wondered about the families living in those beehives. Did they have light? How did they cook? What happened in their crowded rooms at night? I don't claim to be the great philanthropist, but I always asked myself those questions. The children, the fathers, the mothers, the teenagers. They envied us of course, living in England, France, America, the dreamlands of plenty. Unlike the ant on the floor they knew better, at least a tiny bit.

After parking the car I looked at my watch. It was late, but the next day was a holiday. I directed my steps towards Maxim's bar on Kasr el Nil.

Ernest Hemingway described the tavern as the greatest institution devised by man. Maxim's was not a café in Paris or a watering hole on the Florida Keys. It was not a pub in London or a bar filled with early morning drinkers in New York. It was just a melting pot where we gathered later in the day because we were alive and still reasonably young and not yet chronically addicted to television.

I was certainly looking for nothing more than an hour or two of camaraderie as I stepped in from the busy street that night. The young doorman greeted me with a flourish. The deal was that he would teach me a new Arabic phrase each time I came in and I would tip him a twenty piaster piece when I left. The phrase of the day was, "Eftah el bab." Open the door, which of course was his job. I ordered a beer and found that I felt like drinking.

Maxim's was popular with foreigners and locals. Dress was formal by European standards, a suit and tie not uncommon at the bar, but there were no rules. The atmosphere was not formal. We milled around and spoke to anyone using a language we understood.

I spoke to an educated Egyptian who after a while confided that his wife had been unbearable that night. Their children were grown up and she was not the happiest person in the world. Could it be menopause? I told him I thought that was a good possibility. He seemed surprised to have met a civilized person in the bar. I told him he should visit the place more often.

There was an American from New York City. He was the one who told me about the early morning bars where you saw the same individuals at dawn each day drinking whisky on the way to work. What kind of work? I was curious to know. Stockbrokers? Gamblers? He told me that some indeed were track people. Drinking before work instead of after it did not interfere with family life, which I found an interesting thought. He was a film director, just passing through Cairo, he said, meeting my eye. I asked if he knew Martin MacKay, who was making a documentary film on the Yemen or Suez wars or some such thing. He had no knowledge of MacKay and asked about the hammam. Were they all they were cracked up to be? I said I didn't think he would be disappointed.

In spite of thinking back, I cannot identify any other conversation that I had that night. In fact for all the hours I spent in Maxim's bar, the recollections that I have are mostly of a general nature, of the atmosphere rather than particular incidents or conversations. I remember the Egyptian with his menopausal wife and the American with his description of the New York bars not because they were exceptional, but because of what was just about to happen, now only a few hours in the future. Otherwise I'm sure it would have been just another night, adding something to my experience of life no doubt, but leaving no memory.

It was late when I left the bar and headed back to my new and now well-liked apartment. I had no trepidation walking on the Cairo streets. To begin with I'm not a worrier, and in those days I could run. Of that particular

91

walk home I have no memory. I would guess that my thoughts centered on the day's events, Picton leaving for Saigon, and talking to Vermelle about the future. Maybe God knew what was about to happen, but I did not.

CHAPTER TWENTY-ONE

CAIRO
March, 1965

At five a.m. on the morning of Monday 15th March I was wakened by loud banging on the door of my apartment in Midan el Tahrir (Freedom Square) in central Cairo. I was fast asleep, having been in bed for less than an hour but was wakened by banging loud enough to raise the dead. In the hallway I switched on the lights and called out asking who was there.

"Police! Open immediately!"

"Is the building on fire?"

"Open immediately!"

I opened the door and about two dozen men dressed in dark suits poured in. They were led by a short, heavyset man in a black suit whose first words were, "Who is Judy?"

"Judy?" I watched them peel off into different rooms. They seemed to know where they were going. "I don't think I know anyone called Judy. What's going on?"

"Where is the radio?" he asked.

I pointed to the kitchen. "I've got one in the bedroom as well."

"We mean the wireless transmitter."

"What? I don't have one of those," I said, grinning – till a horrible premonition came over me.

They opened the cupboards in the spare bedroom. By now I was explaining that none of what they saw belonged to me. I was keeping it for a friend who was a technician with a film crew. I'd seen the little radio telephones but didn't think it was important. They probably used them for communicating in the desert.

"What is in this suitcase?"

"I don't know. I never opened it."

I did not have a key for the locked suitcase. They opened it. I was still trying to explain that none of this belonged to me when a taller man in a grey suit spoke to the chief. He had notebooks and sheets of paper in his hands.

93

"You know what this is?" I saw lines of numbers and letters on the sheets of paper. "These are codes. And these?"

"I've no idea. I've never seen this stuff."

"These are plans of military installations."

I could not believe it. "Maybe it's something to do with the film they're making."

"Come out here," he said.

In the hallway of my apartment he told me I was under arrest. I was going to be taken with them for questioning. He told me that his name was Mr Aleesh. I would later learn that this was the same senior officer, Hassan Aleesh, who had arrested Wolfgang Lotz three weeks earlier. Lotz described him as being short and fat. I would say heavyset, with dark hair and very shrewd dark eyes. There was no personal hostility at this time. Certainly not from Aleesh. He told me to get dressed and I went into my bedroom and did so, watched by a couple of dark suits. I was aware of them swarming like ants all over the apartment, opening windows and searching the ledges outside. Conversation was in Arabic except when I was being addressed, which was seldom and always by Aleesh.

What went through my mind at that time is not recorded there in detail. I remember sharp exchanges between Aleesh and one of the other senior men. I did not know it at the time but learned later that the arrest was most likely a joint operation between the secret police and the Justice Department. I would later learn that this was also true in the case of Lotz.

There was a piece of strange comedy which I relate because I recall it clearly. Outside of the apartment I was being escorted to the elevator when I discovered that the zipper on my fly was broken. It would not zip up. I remember turning with an embarrassed grin and explaining this to Aleesh who was with a group of men behind me. They had just closed the door of the apartment so that it could not be opened in the usual way. (I learned later that the power and water supply had been turned off as if for a lengthy absence.) Aleesh gave orders and a technical man knelt by the door. A few seconds later, with a flourish, he had it open. I went to my bedroom, escorted as before and donned another pair of slacks.

In going down I think we took the steps, not the elevator. When we stepped out into the early morning light I saw that the street was blocked off and lined with official cars. This was not an alleyway but a main street in central Cairo. I remember gazing at all this and can only assume that I was handcuffed before an audience of pedestrians beyond the police cordon. The truth is I do not recall that either.

Inside one of the cars, I was on the back seat between Mr Aleesh and another man. Aleesh looked me in the eye and spoke directly. "I believe you are innocent," he said. I don't know if it's a tribute to his training or my naiveté but I believed this at the time. "But there are certain procedures we have to follow." I was then blindfolded by the other occupant of the back seat.

My estimate of the time we drove through the streets of Cairo is probably meaningless, but I would say it was in the region of half an hour. From later information, I believe I was driven to the Tura prison, which is located to the south of Cairo, near the corniche that borders the Nile. I remember hearing the sound of soldiers' voices and the clanging of gates. Then I was taken from the car. With hands on my elbows I was led up a flight of steps and then down and along lengthy corridors where there was a kind of silence. A metal door was opened and I was pushed inside. Not roughly. There was no manhandling at this point. The blindfold came off and I saw that I was in a cell.

The dimensions of the cell were small. There was no window and no furniture. Just grey walls and a grey metal door. I stood near the door. In one corner I saw a hole in the stone floor and a water tap. That would be where Muslims could wash themselves and pray. I have no memory of what I was thinking or saying at this juncture. I'm sure I was demanding to be allowed to call the British Embassy, a request which was ignored. I was searched. They took my watch and shoelaces and a set of keys.

It was clear that I was in serious trouble. They thought I was a spy. Whatever happened now would be their decision. I had no power, no rights, no hope.

No reasonable hope. But being who I was I *did* have hope, almost a kind of faith that somehow I would come out of this. It was pretty deep down, but it was there. This was all a mistake. They would realize that and let me go.

A tall Arab in a black coat stepped into the cell beside me. Mr Aleesh and the others stood in the doorway. I was near there with my back to the wall when the tall one moved up close. Our eyes met. I was in no position to resist, but that was no reason to show fear. I recall exactly what was in my mind. At the first blow I would go down against the wall and try to cover my head. That was my instinctive plan.

As a child of eight or nine I was caught and roughed up one day by the Albion Street gang. I went home in tears and told my mother, who asked some questions about their age and said, "Don't cry to me. Go talk to him." Meaning the one who'd mocked me.

I went back out and walked up Albion Street. They were still there, boys and girls, with their leader, who was a few years older than me. They watched with curiosity as I approached. What did the 'Grammar Pup' think he was going to do? I walked up to the leader, my eyes fixed on his. Did I think I could fight him? I threw my right foot as hard as I could into the fork in the short grey pants he wore. I saw his face change as he covered himself and began to go down. I ran like the wind and did not look back till I was in my own building. I don't think any of them followed me. "I kicked him between the legs and ran away," I told my mother. "Good," she said.

At the first blow I would go down against the wall. But not before he started. Then I would do my best to ward off any kicks. After a long stare, he turned to the people in the doorway with a kind of smile. When he did so my eyes jerked that way and met the hard gaze of Mr Aleesh. They were all watching closely. I can believe they had exchanged opinions on how I would react.

Then I was alone. They left, the door was closed, and it was silent in the cell.

There was a small window in the door that could be opened from the outside. I assumed there was a peephole that allowed them to see in. I examined the hole in the corner of the floor. Above it a narrow passage led to what seemed to be open air not too far above. I saw sky, but there was no way of scaling that tunnel to whatever lay above. It was the only source of light in the cell.

I walked around, thinking. So far so good, I told myself. I had not cowered when threatened. They had all the cards, but I had that small victory. What they were doing was routine to them. To me it was a new world and I was alone. So far I had not been beaten up or tortured. That was all I knew for now. So far so good. What was in the future was in the future.

I believe you are innocent.

I believed him when he said that. And it was the truth. But that didn't mean they would not be playing with my mind. There was going to be interrogation. That much was clear and the sooner the better so far as I was concerned. But then, if they did not hear what they wanted to hear, what next?

For a while, I did little more than look at the grey walls. From the party in my flat to this, in a little more than twenty-four hours. To this point I'd had little chance to do much more than react. For all the warnings I'd been given, it was an unforeseen event. Preventable maybe. Reversible, no. I was here, in this cell, and that was it.

Then I began to think.

CHAPTER TWENTY-TWO

At the time I was arrested, the confessed Israeli spy Wolfgang Lotz and his wife were also in custody and being interrogated in Cairo. They were arrested on Monday, February 22nd, three weeks prior to my arrest on Monday March 15th. According to Lotz's later account (in *The Champagne Spy*, published by St. Martin's press in 1972) the secret police searched his villa in Giza, an upscale district on Gezira Island, and found a transmitter radio hidden in a set of bathroom scales. Faced with such damning evidence Lotz confessed, and now the hunt was on for his accomplices.

With the knowledge I have now I feel pretty sure that Lotz was not able to identify any Mossad professionals in Egypt. The Egyptians obviously felt the same since he was not subjected to physical coercion but appeared on television prior to a public trial. His wife, Waltraud, on the other hand was subjected to coercion in the form of being left lying in cold water until she was ready to speak. Lotz claimed that she told them nothing, and in fact it seems unlikely that she knew much more than he did. They met on a train in Europe shortly after he had agreed to work for Israel. They were married within weeks in spite of the fact that he already had a wife and child in Paris. Egyptian logic had it that they were brought together by the Israeli Mossad so that she could help him in his mission, and I think that's probably true. In retrospect I see them as sayanim – civilians who work with the Mossad for reasons of patriotism and perhaps financial advantage.

At the time of my arrest I had given little thought to any of this, but that soon changed. Sitting in the cell, looking at the walls and wondering about my future, I now gave it serious consideration.

It wasn't hard to guess that Lotz and his wife were being asked what they knew about me. If they possessed information that would endanger a compatriot I assumed they would try not to give it, but what about me? They might even be the reason that I was sitting in this cell.

Hans Goslich contacted me after the arrest of Lotz and his wife. By that time they were in custody and unable to be reached even by the tendrils of the Mossad. But hold on. Martin MacKay had left Egypt before the arrests. In the scary scenario that he was an Israeli spy, he could have planted information before or after leaving Cairo which was communicated to the Lotzes.

Why?

To distract the Egyptians while important people were getting out.

I recalled the line of cars outside my building. I thought of the planning that must have gone into the raid and the possibly weeks of surveillance that preceded it. It might seem like the plot of a spy thriller, but I couldn't help wondering if MacKay or some other operative had informed Lotz that an individual who was not part of their organization had been compromised. Before he was arrested Lotz would say nothing of this to anyone. But after his arrest, when being pressed for the names of accomplices, he came up with the name Norman Lang. While people like Goslich and maybe others were getting out, the Egyptians were watching and closing in on me.

I thought of this but still could not believe it. Mackay was certainly not your typical expatriate. Vermelle was not the only one who had looked askance at him. Plenty of money and no visible job? A film company working in the desert – cheek to jowl with Nasser's secret rocket ranges? Was MacKay even his real name? Did he look Jewish? Actually, he did.

In the cell I did a lot of pacing and staring at the walls. My mind was too occupied to register details, but I think the floor was split-level which gave me a cold seat of sorts. I sat thinking of the Nabokov novel about a prisoner who became a chess champion by mentally studying the game while in solitary confinement. That day I had plenty of other things to think about.

I had a vague picture in my mind of Wolfgang Lotz as a man with what looked like a brown squirrel sitting on his head. This came from a photograph I had seen in the *Al Ahram* offices. I could picture him saying, "Yes, we got Lang a job at the Madrasa el Nasr. He's a trained physicist and if you care to look you'll find he's circumcised. They recruited him in Paris, where he lived for a year. Why else do you think he came to Egypt? To educate your future leaders?"

Was that possible? And if so, would Mr Aleesh be fooled? Lotz later portrayed Hassan Aleesh as a kind of buffoon, which did not match my estimation. But even in those innocent days, back in the sixties when notions like truth and honesty still existed, reality and truth were only factors in the equation. The Egyptians had enough evidence against me that even my mother would believe I had been spying. They would decide whatever they wanted to decide and do what suited their political leaders.

In time I became convinced that they knew what they would find when they raided my apartment. They had probably been in the place and searched it as they had with Lotz. So what brought me to their attention in the first place?

Mooney? Picton? Vermelle?

Had I babbled to others?

No, and no.

How then?

In Lotz's case they had detected his transmissions. Then they arrested him and someone pointed them in my direction.

Goslich?

MacKay?

I just could not believe it. Maybe a stray word from me or someone else had gotten around or been picked up by the ubiquitous surveillance on foreigners. Whatever the case, things looked black for me. I had to face the possibility that my goose was cooked. So how could I make the best of it?

To begin with, I was innocent. And Aleesh was no fool. My best and maybe only strategy was to convince them of that and hope for the best.

CHAPTER TWENTY-THREE

I could write a book of some length on the things that went through my mind in the next few hours. And that would be only what I remember. It takes thousands of words to describe an experience that can visit the memory in a second or two. I found myself thinking of other altercations with authority.

In my last year of high school I worked in a Butlin's Holiday Camp in the town of Ayr near Glasgow. A couple of friends were Charles Wright, who became a distinguished medical man, and Derek Campbell, an Edinburgh man a few years older than us who was taking a Bachelor of Commerce degree. Charlie was a classmate of mine at Paisley Grammar. One night towards the end of the summer we decided to steal Billy Butlin's bust. This was a pompous eyesore of a thing which sat in state in one of the administration buildings.

During the day in question I entered the building on some pretext and left a window slightly open. The plan was that we would come back at night when the camp was asleep and remove the bust, which sat on a pedestal on a small stage. When the time came the other two had reservations. I berated them for wanting to chicken out and they agreed to go through with it.

It was long after midnight when I entered the locked building. I used a table knife to unlatch the window and climbed in. Only now did I realize that a lighted back room was not empty. There were voices coming from it. It was a Sunday night and the week's take was being prepared for transfer by armored truck the next morning. I reported this at the open window. They said, "Let's come back tomorrow night." I said, "Let's see." The streets of the camp were deserted. It was a good time if I could be quiet about lifting the bust.

I then found that the terra cotta bust was bolted to the wooden pedestal. It was not heavy. Even the pedestal was flimsy, but the combination was too bulky to go through the window. I listened to the quiet voices in the back room.

They seemed absorbed. I reported at the window that I was going to have to make some noise. If worse came to worst we should be ready to make a fast getaway. They told me I was crazy but stayed at the window.

I tried to gently wrestle Billy Butlin from his roost. No luck. Finally I swung the thing and broke off the pedestal against the stage. I ran to the window, passed the bust to my friends and climbed out. No reaction from within. They put a coat over the bust and we ran with it through the empty streets.

A hedge separated a field of cows from the camp. We crossed a flowerbed close to the main gate, which was closed and unmanned, shoved the bust through the hedge and concealed it as best we could. We then made it back to our quarters undetected.

The next day it was all over camp. The local security chief and even Billy Butlin himself appealed for information to the campers and all who worked there. Then came the offer of amnesty if the bust were returned. It was probably a student prank and still on the camp they said, and if it were returned there would be no consequences. Then came the ultimatum. Return the bust or the police would be called and the perpetrators charged with breaking and entering. The next day the police were on the campsite.

In the meantime most of the holiday-makers loved it. The kitchen and bartending and other staff talked of nothing else. I remember some tough guys from Glasgow hinting that they had knowledge of the affair and me asking them questions that showed they didn't. Amazingly the thing remained lying just outside of the camp and a week later when the other perpetrators and I were leaving to go back to school, it had still not been found.

By this time the incident was national news. The enraged Billy Butlin threatened no mercy for the perpetrators, who would be apprehended and punished to the full extent of the law. To our amazement the bust was still not found. It was weeks later when we decided to bring it to Glasgow.

A friend of ours called Tom Downey, another classmate, found the rotor arm that his father had removed from the family car and also a set of keys. We got the car going and although none of us could drive properly, we managed to get it to the field of cows outside the camp in the middle of the night. Knowing roughly where we'd left the thing we entered the field and moved along the hedge.

Cows are curious animals. Also quite large. They certainly wanted to know what we were doing in their field at night. Surrounded by their looming shadows, we found the bust and got it to the car.

For the next few months this piece of sculpture lay under my bed in our home in Endrick Drive in Paisley. My parents knew of it and wisely said nothing since "The Pinching of Billy Butlin's Bust" was still an open case and the threat of prosecution had not been removed. Eventually we gave the bust to some students at Glasgow Art School who used it for whatever purpose, before it ended up in the River Kelvin.

Glasgow students could be quite inventive when it came to pranks against figures of authority. A car belonging to a professor who had irritated some engineering students was found on the roof of a three story campus building one morning. A political guest whose name was Dick Mabon was giving a spiel that was not universally popular in the debating hall one day when a large fish, several feet long and weighing many pounds, appeared from a balcony above the stage. Attached to a cable that went across the hall to the balcony on the other side, this was noticed waving in the air above the stage, and caused a jocular remark or two till the fish swooped down and scattered the platform party.

Prior to the bust incident, which was local and humorous, there was a historically significant national incident involving the Stone of Scone, otherwise known as the Stone of Destiny, on which Scottish kings had been crowned in the town of Scone until the late thirteenth century, when it was taken by the forces of Edward I and removed to Westminster Abbey in London, where it was used to crown English and later British kings. On Christmas Day 1950, a small group of Edinburgh and Glasgow students (one of whom was the brother of a close friend of mine, Kenneth Stuart) retrieved the guarded stone (which was chained to the floor, weighed over three hundred pounds, and which they did without inflicting harm on the policeman who guarded it) and spirited it back to Scotland in spite of the best efforts of Scotland Yard to stop them. (Details of this can be found on the Internet.)

I know that many things went through my mind in those few hours. Thoughts and reminiscences of past exploits from another life. Young people will take risks that the devil himself would balk at. But behind it all we knew there was a justice system with a sense of fairness and even a sense of humor in the country of our birth. We would not just disappear or be held at the whim of politicians. That of course was then, not now. And this was Egypt. But my background gave me the strength of hope and the fact that I was innocent would surely count for something.

After a while – it could have been an hour or several hours – I began to think about what I would say to my interrogators.

CHAPTER TWENTY-FOUR

I have always felt that the Egyptians made one major mistake in dealing with me: they gave me time to think. In general this may be good strategy. Weaken the prisoner with sleep deprivation and the like and give him or her a chance to face the grim reality and perhaps decide to cooperate. That may work in many cases with a prisoner who is guilty. In my case it gave me time not only to get my story straight, but to decide what I would say and what I would not say.

First, I took a major decision about my attitude toward Goslich and MacKay. As for Goslich I would show some resentment because he had left me with his questionable possessions. I would not assume he was a spy because that is so far from my world that I wouldn't even think of it and I would make the following point. If I were a spy holding spy gear for whatever reason, would I mention it to other people like Vermelle, Mooney, Picton? Obviously not. The proof follows. I am not a spy.

As for MacKay, I would display no suspicion and no resentment. I would not see him as a possible leaker of information to the likes of Lotz, either through coded communications from Tel Aviv or any other way, because I was too innocent even to think of that. I developed that thought in detail.

Martin MacKay was just a pal who was nice enough to have lent me his car while he was out of town. I knew almost nothing about his job or other activities for none of that was of much interest to me. I knew where he lived. I'd been to his house in Heliopolis and had spoken to his servant but couldn't remember his name (it was Joseph). I knew where his dog was because he gave me that information. (I thought about that and could see no problem for the family who had it.) As for his claims to Scottish aristocracy and some babble about Drumnadrochit Castle I would not acknowledge having heard that. (If it was a cover, I still wonder with amusement who thought it up.) He went to school in

Edinburgh and had been in the RAF. I could not deny
having met some people through him, but I would play it
down. I was terrible with names. Maybe I would recall a
few first names but no addresses. And a few harmless
stories about meeting strangers, to whom he could be very
charming by the way. At the airport when I saw him off,
there was an American family the mother of which was
ready to engage him as a tutor for her children if he would
consider doing such work when he came back. She was
convinced that "this young man" – her words – would be an
excellent mentor for her son. I remember wondering about
that. This kind of story I could tell. I would mention his
love of animals (which I doubted). Nothing they could use.
Like the fact that he was smuggling gems out of Egypt. I
still wonder if he really did that or was testing me in some
way.

Given time to think, those were my decisions. I would
act in all innocence towards MacKay because that would
make me look more innocent myself. The less I said the
less chance of unearthing something that could reflect on
me. I have said I was innocent, not stupid.

There was also a funny thing that probably smacks of
prejudice. As I paced around in the small cell my fingers
literally itched to get around the neck beneath the pale
round face of Hans Goslich. But in spite of serious
suspicions, I did not feel that way about my compatriot
Martin MacKay. If he really were a British or Israeli spy,
motivated by whatever, he was just doing what he had to
do to get out and help his associates to do the same. I
should not take it personally. I just happened to be there.

I have often said to opinionated people (unlike myself, of
course) that I am not responsible for what I believe or feel.
What I do or say is a different matter. I do not deny that
thoughts can lead to actions, and in this case my
instinctive thoughts were about to do just that. I was going
to lie to the interrogators.

CHAPTER TWENTY-FIVE

Time was impossible to measure in the cell. It could have been an hour or two or even more before I rapped on the window of the door. As it opened, I saw a pair of eyes.

"This is not right," I said. "I want to call the British Embassy and inform them that I have been arrested. This is all a big mistake. I am innocent and there isn't enough air in this cell."

He finally opened the door. It was not my right to call the embassy, the plainclothes guard explained. The embassy would be informed in due course by Egyptian authorities. I could see that he was not a prison guard. He was dressed like those who had arrested me, though less formally. Instead of a suit he wore a casual coat and slacks. Interesting protocol.

I argued about the conventions. Leaning in the doorway of the cell, which I relished being out of even partly, I insisted that it was my right to be taken to a telephone. I was looking for any excuse to get out of there even for a few minutes. The guard was civil. He seemed almost sympathetic. But another one who came by was anything but. He told me sharply that I had no rights. They had enough evidence against me to have me shot. He ordered me back into the cell. I remember looking down at him. He was not a tall man but that was not the issue. He was hostile but did not raise his hands. By this time I was beginning to sense something. It began to seem that they were under orders to be careful how they treated me. That was an encouraging thought – or was it? Lotz was also being treated in accordance with international law but only because they wanted a public trial after which he might be executed. They had almost the same evidence against me as they had against him.

Back in the cell I began to chafe. I felt I had figured out the best way to handle the situation. Now I just wanted to get on with it and find out where I stood. Time passed.

I rapped on the door again. The window was opened by the civil guard. They had taken my cigarettes I said. I wanted a cigarette. He passed a Belmont cigarette through the small window and offered me a light. I couldn't smoke in here I said. There wasn't enough air. He glanced around to see who was in the corridor and opened the door so that I could stand in it and smoke.

Did they really have so much evidence against me? I asked. What could they have except a couple of things that had been left with me by someone I scarcely knew?

He was not at liberty to say. But they knew everything about me he said. I would learn that in due course.

Standing in the doorway there wasn't much to see except the doors of other cells, but there were sounds. I heard the distant screaming of a prisoner. That would not be me, I thought. I had heard that one of their tortures is a dentist's chair in which they bore holes in your teeth. Could I keep silent during that? I would scream silently, I told myself.

But I wanted to be taken to a telephone. There had to be international law. Even if I were a spy, which I was not, I still had rights. And I didn't say it, but I really wanted out of the damned cell. It was getting cold. Oddly enough, I do not believe I asked for food. I had no hunger and no thirst. I suppose there was a supply of water in the cell though I don't remember using it. I don't think I urinated either.

Alone again inside the cell I looked up the chimney to the sky. Was it darker than before? There was no electricity and no light. After a while I rapped on the door again.

I needed a mattress and a blanket. There was nothing in here. I'd had no sleep the night before. Even a prison cell must have a mattress.

That was not true, I was told. This was a prison cell and it did not have a mattress. I had no right to a mattress. I heard impatient voices outside, but I did not give up. I wanted a mattress and I had a reason for it.

It had dawned on me that I was being kept awake deliberately. Always ready to accept a good sign, I took this as an indication that I would be interrogated before too long. But what did that mean? Hours? Days? I wanted to accelerate the process.

I rapped on the door repeatedly. It was not opened but I went on demanding a mattress. This was inappropriate behavior I told them through the door. So far I had not been treated badly. They were justified in wanting to question me even though it was all a big mistake. But it was wrong to leave me in a cell where I could not even lie down. That was inhumane.

No response. But with only one card to play I went on playing it. If they didn't want me to sleep I would pretend to sleep. I knew that they could see me through a peephole in the door. I tried lying on the stone floor and pretending to sleep, but it was difficult to stay still for long. I kept demanding a mattress.

I know I thought about my parents in Scotland at this time. They would be distraught if they knew what was happening. How and when would they find out? And my friends in Cairo. They would hear about it pretty soon if they didn't know already. I thought about Vermelle, with whom I had been discussing the future only hours before. Was she safe? How strange it all seemed. I can't report all that went through my mind. I wish I could remember it. All I know for sure is that I wanted to get to the next step even if it meant torture.

We have all seen movies of people chained to dungeon walls. I had never given it much thought, but that obviously could not go on indefinitely. There is solitary confinement. But at least the person has a bed in which to sleep, to dream, and there has to be a routine to the day with meals, exercise, some words with a bored jailor. Regular prison was a common enough experience. Some said it was hell, some said not so bad. I've heard men of principle, such as Jack Kevorkian, say that prison is not bad if you know you're innocent – meaning I guess that the people around you know that too. But this wasn't just prison. This was being arrested and accused of spying in a time of war. In that case innocence or guilt, according to some, is trumped by national security.

For some length of time they ignored my rapping on the door. I bruised my knuckles doing it. I was never a good complainer. Very seldom in my adult life had I asked anyone for the same thing twice. But at this time my whole being was focused on getting a mattress.

CHAPTER TWENTY-SIX

I remember where I was standing in the cell when the door was opened. More precisely, I was probably sitting on the split-level and rose when they came in carrying the mattress. They put it on the floor and dropped a ragged blanket beside it. Still no indication of what was going to happen or when. I'm sure I asked, but there was no communication. No smiles, no threats. But now I had won another little victory. I had a mattress.

The mattress was thin but just about adequate. I lay on it with my back to the door and pulled the thin blanket over me. This was comfort. Warmth and some rest for the first time in what seemed like ages. I remember the gist of what went through my mind.

I had never in my life been further from sleep. Instead I rehearsed again what I would say during the interrogation and what I could safely omit. MacKay had never said much about what he did with his aircraft. In the circumstances one had to think of its potential for spotting military bases and missile sites, but I wouldn't mention that. I thought carefully of what I would say about people I had met through him and certain opinions that I would keep to myself. It reminded me of lying in bed at home the night before a test or examination and rehearsing facts that I would need the next day. I did not have a photographic memory, but I could produce a prepared statement word for word.

Again it's hard to estimate time. I don't even recall taking note of the changing light patterns from the tunnel to the roof. But I know that I was wide awake and had not been on the mattress for too long before the cell door was abruptly opened.

This is it, I thought. The moment of truth. I cannot describe the feeling of relief that flooded through me.

CHAPTER TWENTY-SEVEN

None of the senior men were in the doorway. I looked for the sympathetic guard, but he must have gone off duty. They told me that I had to be blindfolded before walking through the corridors. I said that was perfectly fine and rejoiced inwardly. We were leaving the cell.

I don't believe it was by design, but at one point we passed close to a person who was being dragged along the corridor. We were close enough that I could almost smell his fear, and his pleading voice was in my ear. I still have a mental picture of the man I didn't see being dragged like a donkey with its legs stiff. Walking blind I wanted to raise my hands in front of my face but just had to trust them as they guided me by the elbows.

When the blindfold came off I was in a room with a table and a chair. I recall greenish walls and I might have been escorted to a toilet. Seated at the table I was supplied with paper and the closest thing to a weapon that I had held since my arrest, a pencil. Very focused on the task in hand, more so than on the people around me, I listened as I was told what I had to do. I was to write my statement, explaining why I had come to Egypt and what I was doing there. They wanted to know every detail of how that had been arranged. They also wanted my personal history as an adult and the details of my life in Cairo. I was to take my time. There was no rush. They wanted details of how I came to be in possession of a radio transmitter.

A radio transmitter! What were they talking about? Those little radio telephones might allow people to speak to each other from a few miles away, but I didn't have a radio transmitter.

They didn't argue. While my mind went on a rollercoaster, wondering what they had found in the suitcase that I never opened, they told me very seriously that I must write every detail and it must be the truth. If I lied they would know and it would not go well for me. By this time I was pretty sure that the Justice Department was involved in my arrest as we had guessed it was in the

111

case of Lotz. Did that mean that torture was not on the agenda? I didn't think of that too much. I just went from moment to moment.

A radio transmitter! Was that possible? I began to think of practicalities. They should be able to determine that no transmissions were made from my apartment. But what they knew and what they said did not have to correspond. I shook off these thoughts. This was no time for panic. Right now what I had to do was write my statement and every word of it had to be the truth (except for what I wouldn't say).

For the next period of time I was so focused on this that I cannot even describe how I was watched or guarded in the room. Was I offered food? I don't know. I'm sure I did not eat. There was probably water on the table. There was probably at least one guard not far from me at all times. What I recall is writing everything I had been asked to write. I even have a kind of image of myself doing it while sitting at the table. And thank God for forethought. I had no way to edit or erase what I put down.

Putting things into words had never been my problem. I described my plan for seeing something of the world before doing a research degree. Itinerant teaching was a convenient way of doing this. (It was also a common cover for operatives, I would later learn.) I had lived in Paris and London and traveled in Spain and Switzerland. I picked Cairo as a place to visit in the Middle East because of its history and wrote to the Egyptian cultural attaché. I was offered a job and air tickets were provided. I described teaching at the school and living there for a few months before taking an apartment in the city. I met Martin MacKay in the sporting club in Heliopolis. We became good friends and as time went by I met other Europeans and Americans. I did some socializing with people at the school but apart from that mostly with other foreigners. The Americans I knew tended to be government officials and were mostly married. Vermelle was an exception. By now I knew they must have seen her come and go from my apartment. The Europeans tended to be single, like myself. A good number of them heterosexually challenged, but not spies. We met in restaurants and bars and at parties, and I had visited most of the sporting clubs but was a member of none of them. I described meeting Goslich and agreeing to keep some possessions for him. I had seen the stuff in his boxes and knew it was illegal but had not felt compelled to get rid of it. My conscience was clear. I was not a spy and hoped this misunderstanding would soon be over. I wrote down what I had planned to say about people I met through MacKay. Through Goslich I truthfully said I had met no one. This was my signed statement, and if they had other questions I would be happy to answer them in whatever detail they required.

Back in the cell I lay on the mattress and waited. With my back to the door I went over every word I had written. I was sure that there was nothing there that could be proved false or used against me. The omitted facts were not all in the defense of other people. If I mentioned taking MacKay to the airport with contraband gems for example, I was making myself an accessory to a crime. If I fingered people like his servant and others, who could predict what they might come up with about me when being dragged along the corridors outside? I genuinely had no wish to make trouble for others but was also in a tight spot myself.

There is another point I mulled. The seemingly innocent question, What made you come to Egypt in the first place? was actually quite loaded. Not counting married men who had been assigned there through their government jobs, ninety percent of the foreign males visiting Cairo were homosexual. Of the other ten percent, like Hans Goslich, Martin MacKay, Wolfgang Lotz and myself, I won't say that three out of four were spies, but that may not have been too much of an exaggeration.

What else did I think about lying in the cell, while giving the impression that I was asleep? I am very aware of one recurring thought.

CHAPTER TWENTY-EIGHT

In the situation I was in the possibility of torture was very real. After the first threats there had been no overt intimidation, but the hints were loud and clear.

We have enough evidence against you to have you shot.

Indeed. And what happens when you don't find more? Or less than you expected?

If you don't tell us what we need to know, we have ways of learning what we need to know.

There had been mention of the dentist's chair.

Most people have imagined being tortured. We can think of the vague horror, but the imagination balks when it comes to details. Traumatic injury shocks us into unconsciousness. But how does the brain deal with deliberately inflicted pain or even the threat of it? Does rational thought remain?

While lying on the hard-won mattress and pretending to sleep, I had the unpleasant thought that I was like a poker player with no cards. Unlike a real spy – Wolfgang Lotz, for example – I had nothing to confess. Being innocent, I didn't even have a well-prepared "confession" that I could bring out bit by bit – as would Martin MacKay, for example, if he were a spy and were captured – to give them something to think about and make the torturers feel they had done their job. All I could do was go on repeating what I'd already told them. How do you prove that you are not what you are not?

Beyond that, I didn't care to question. There was nothing to be gained and it would certainly do nothing to ease my mind. I was ready for the worst in a deep-down way, but simply didn't go along that road. I just hoped for the best, and there was actually a hopeful little incident that I have not related. While snapping at me and ordering me back into the cell with implied threats, the hostile guard was also speaking in Arabic to the other one. After what sounded like a question, the answer he received included the word "nada" which he repeated in surprise. "Nada?" Nothing? – with his eyes on me. Always the

optimist, I took this to mean that they had not yet come up
with anything conclusive against me.

I believe you are innocent.

We have enough evidence against you to have you shot.

We know everything about you. Everything.

Nada.

So what did I think when the door was suddenly opened
yet again?

I thought, good! I was right. They don't want me
sleeping. And this time, this is it.

CHAPTER TWENTY-NINE

Once again I was being led blindfolded through the corridors. But now there was a difference: we were going up. That was a good sign. Torture chambers would be down, right? The guards gave me no indication one way or the other.

We entered a room and I sensed the presence of people. I was made to sit on a stool which turned out to be in the middle of the floor. When the mask came off I found myself bathed in light. There were three classical arc lights above a desk behind which I could see nothing. I turned and looked behind me. Seated with his knees crossed and a huge semiautomatic in one hand was the same tall Arab who had acted as though he was about to attack me in the cell. My eyes went from the gun to his face and he gave an almost sheepish grin. His manner seemed to say, "Don't worry. I know you're not going to jump up and attack anybody, but this is what we do." Behind him in the L-shaped room a man wearing dark glasses and a blue blazer sat at a machine that looked like a form of typewriter. He was a stenographer. Other people were behind him out of the direct glare of the lights. It was an interrogation room. I faced the lights, trying to see behind them. Although deprived of rest I was wide awake and could not have swallowed a morsel of food if it were offered to me. I wasn't even greatly bothered by the lights. And it may seem odd but I cannot swear to it whether I was handcuffed or not. My feeling is that I was not. I was isolated in the chair. Alone with the lights and the large weapon behind me. I remember very well the first question that came from behind the lights.

"Now tell us how you met Wolfgang Lotz."

I actually laughed. I think it was a reflex to being asked something that was meant to shock me after all the thinking I had done about it. It did not mean I was either amused or unaware of what might lie ahead of me.

I told them I could not be sure whether I had met Lotz or his wife. If I did it was without knowing who they were or remembering anything about it. I had met the occasional German and some horse people and seen them around in places like the sporting clubs. But I did not move much in those circles and knew none of the people beyond possibly having a drink with them at the bar. And while we were at it, I assured them, I was not spying for Israel or any other country.

That was the start of an interrogation which lasted many hours. At the time I estimated about fourteen hours, but that's a guess based on the approximate time of day when it was over. Because of the lights I could see none of the inquisitors and did not recognize any of their voices. Sometimes I thought I might be listening to Mr Aleesh but could not know for sure. I know that the questioners came and went for the voices changed from time to time and I could sense movement behind the lights. But I did not keep track of personnel changes in the room. Whatever the exact number of hours, it was a marathon.

In the account that follows I have put into dialogue some of the exchanges that took place. In doing so, once again, I cannot claim that the words would correspond to the transcript that was taken. If I were able to gain access to that document, I would use it. All I can claim is that the gist and tenor of the exchanges described below are as close as I can make them.

CHAPTER THIRTY

The different voices came from behind the lights. I could hear the small changes of direction and answered as though meeting the unseen eyes that studied me. After the abrupt question about Lotz, they started by going over some personal history.

"What exactly is the degree you have from Glasgow University?"

"It's a double honors in Nat. Phil. and Maths."

"Nat. Phil.?"

"Physics."

"You have a degree in both subjects?"

"It's a combined degree for people interested in theoretical physics. The same combination is offered at Cambridge, which is where Professor Dee at Glasgow University had been before. It might be unique to these two universities."

"So you are a very qualified scientist."

I shrugged.

"You then went to Paris for a year."

"Yes. I wanted some time off before doing a Ph.D."

"And you were teaching English?"

"Yes. I was assistant d'anglais at the Lycée Condorcet."

"Which is the old school of Jean Paul Sartre?"

"Yes."

"Did you meet Sartre?"

"No. But I saw him in a restaurant once when he came in with Simone de Beauvoir. The place went completely quiet. I remember that she ate like a Frenchman."

"What does that mean?"

"Not quietly. The French are more interested in food than in table manners."

"What was the name of the restaurant?"

"The Falstaff."

I sensed that they were trying to get me to relax and wondered what was coming. They had obviously read my statement and done some background checking, as the next questions showed.

"Why do you think he refused the Nobel Prize for Literature?"

"That hadn't happened then."

"When he did, why did he refuse?"

"I'm sure it was political. He didn't want to be beholden."

"To whom?"

"To the West. America. He admired communism."

"How do you feel about communism?"

"It's a beautiful ideal, with the wrong people running it of course. Maybe someday."

"You have some very educated knowledge and ideals. When did you decide to spy for Israel?"

"I never did."

"Why did you come to Egypt?"

"As I said. To teach and see the country."

"What did you wish to see about the country?"

I almost gave a facetious answer but remembered where I was. "I am always interested in other countries. How people live."

After a while a different and less neutral voice came in. "Are you surprised if we find it interesting that a person with your scientific training should happen to be in Egypt at this time?"

"Interesting? I'm not sure what you mean."

"Don't play innocent. You know that there is military work of an important scientific nature being done in our country at this time."

"I do now. I didn't know that when I came."

"Oh, really? You were unaware that we are building rockets to strike back at Israel?"

"I don't think many people in Europe know that."

"So you just woke up one morning and decided to come here? At a time when many people are very anxious to know what we are doing?"

"Actually, that's just about what happened. I've always been interested in the history. The pyramids, the civilization that goes way back. I never gave much thought to Suez or Israel."

"You just want to teach our children?" No answer. "Because you admire our history. Are you a homosexual?"

119

I might have sighed. I hate people who sigh. "No."

"Not at all?"

"I don't know what you mean by that."

"You spent your first months living in the school."

"That's right. Till I got to know my way around Cairo."

"Have you been to the hammam?"

I nodded resignedly. They could have been watching me at that time. "Yes."

"Now why would you do that? A rich European who can bathe in your own luxury apartment?

"I had some friends who were going there that night. I tagged along."

"Your friends had need of a bath?" No answer. "That is a question. When I ask a question, you will answer."

"I guess they like the place because they're homosexual. Like other men go to strip clubs. I went out of curiosity."

"And walked around naked amongst the naked young men?"

"I guess so." I might have laughed. As I might have mentioned, this can happen when it doesn't suit my purpose.

"Answer this carefully. Did you touch any of these boys?"

I thought before answering. "Absolutely not. Not in the sense you mean. And what has this got to do with anything?" I'm sure it is due to this line of questioning that I have to this day an image of the boy on the steps of the pool in the hammam.

Around that time there was a welcome change of voice. The attempt to put me off stride was pretty blatant but not harmless. I had no wish to give them cause to accuse me of something that was commonplace but still a punishable offence. I began to feel as though I were walking on eggs.

"I am interested in your scientific knowledge," one of the voices said. "In the last war, German scientists were able to launch rockets that reached London. How did they do that?"

"You mean, how did they aim a ballistic missile?"

"What is ballistic?"

"No engine. Like firing a bullet."

"Very good. How do you fire a bullet in the air so that it comes down on a target hundreds of miles away?"

I thought about it with the knowledge I had then. Not guessing that this would become part of my profession in the future, I answered while thinking as I went along. "If you know the launch speed and direction, which can be done with gyroscopes. And the position, of course. And you have good models for the effects of air resistance and maybe gravity at different heights. Maybe the rotation of the earth. You should be able to calculate quite accurately where the missile will come down."

"How accurately?"

"Oh, I don't know. It depends on your instruments. They were aiming at a city the size of London. Which was still good engineering at the time. I don't know about hitting a military installation, if that's what you mean."

"Do you think it can be done?"

"I couldn't say. In theory, yes. You have to ask your experts."

"We can ask our experts," the insinuating voice said, "and they will tell us because we pay them. But if you or someone like you asks them just because you're interested, they won't talk much, will they? Unless you can gain their confidence and have the knowledge to put together what they say."

"I wouldn't know. I've never tried."

"Of course not. You are just an innocent school teacher. But if you got friendly with a homosexual German scientist and asked him how his work on the guidance system was going, he might tell you more than he realizes after a drink or two, no?"

"I wouldn't know."

"Do you speak German?"

"No. And I've never even met one of the scientists."

"You have told us that you did. In the country clubs."

"Not knowingly. And if so we never discussed guidance systems."

"Then why do we find you in possession of secret codes and a radio transmitter?"

I protested in exasperation. "I never saw a radio transmitter! I've never used one in my life! If there was a radio transmitter, why didn't you show it to me at the time like you did the other things?"

"Are you calling us liars?"

"And to communicate with Tel Aviv I'd need an aerial. I saw you search outside my windows. Did you find an aerial?" As I asked this I realized the pointlessness of it. They could say what they liked. I began to feel the room closing in.

"Let's go back to an earlier point," one of them said. "When you woke up one morning and decided to come to Egypt, you wrote to our cultural attaché. You told him you were interested in teaching in the Cairo area and supplied him with information which he assumed was true."

"It's all true."

"So you came to Cairo and took up residence in the school. You would seem to have had some teaching experience. During those early weeks you looked for places within walking distance of the school where you could have a glass of beer in the evening. On weekends you took the train into Cairo and went to places frequented by foreigners. How did you meet Martin MacKay?"

By the time he got to the question my heart had slowed a little. Mention of MacKay put me all the way back on guard.

"A teacher at the school took me to one of the sporting clubs. Someone introduced me to Martin."

"You became friends."

"Yes."

"You went to bars and parties. He showed you around Cairo."

"Pretty well. I also met people on my own."

"You have given us a list of friends. Mostly from the universities and embassies."

"And some journalists."

"Didn't you meet people through MacKay?"

"He introduced me to some people. Not many. He spent a lot of his time working."

At this point I was tense and listening closely. I could see nothing through the lights but listened to every little sound that came from behind them. In retrospect I don't think they needed a lie detector to know that I was being less than forthcoming at this time.

"What was MacKay doing in Cairo?"

"As I've said, I never really knew that. He worked for a company called Investrade. They were making some kind of film. That's about all I know."

"What kind of film?"

I can see myself running my fingers through my hair. "I think it was something to do with the wars in Yemen. Or Suez. He talked about being with the RAF at the time of Suez."

"How did you meet Hans Goslich?"

"I think it was in Maxim's bar. He was there one night."

"What did you talk about?"

"I don't recall. Nothing much. I hardly knew the man."

"Did you ever fly with MacKay in his plane?"

"I never did. I never even saw his plane."

"Have you visited his house?"

"Oh, yes."

"And met people there?"

"In a passing way. Usually there was just his servant."

"What is the name of his servant?"

"As I've said, I don't remember that. He was a kind of pudgy, balding guy. I might have heard his name but I don't remember it."

"We think you are lying," one of the calmer voices said.

"I'm sorry. I don't catch names the way some people do."

"Your friend MacKay left his car with you. Why with you and not one of his work colleagues?"

"That's a good question. I was just happy that he picked me."

"Do you think he's coming back to Egypt?"

"I never doubted it till now. I assume so."

"He has a dog."

"Wolfy." I shook my head. It was always a puzzle to me that MacKay had taken on a dog.

"Who is feeding it now and taking it for walks? Joseph?"

"Oh, no." I caught myself. "Yes, that could be the servant's name. Joseph. But the dog is with an English family as I told you."

I remember staring at the lights before one of the voices spoke matter-of-factly. "You have told us very little about this close friend of yours, who is also a Scotsman, and who trusted you enough to leave his car with you. Now I want you to think very hard. I want you to describe, one by one, or couple by couple, all the people you met through Martin MacKay. I want you to give us their names and where they live and everything you know about them. Take your time. We are in no hurry. Search your memory and tell us everything you know."

This was a part of the interrogation I did not relish, but at least I was prepared. Without contradicting anything I had written, or adding anything substantial, I talked around all the social contacts with MacKay, claiming not to remember names and addresses and even mixing some physical descriptions. It was a pretty elaborate deceit, but even if they caught me out I reckoned I could claim I was confused and intimidated. At the end of it I think my questioners were as exhausted as I was and I was told we were going to have a short break.

CHAPTER THIRTY-ONE

Again the blindfold and the corridors. I urinated somewhere without the blindfold being removed. I think I was offered coffee and accepted. Also I believe there was bread of some sort, which was the first food I had eaten since the morning before. The guards leading me were noncommittal. Neither responsive to my weak attempts at humor, nor hostile. I kept thinking that they had enough evidence against me to prove me guilty to the world. My fate depended not on the truth, or on what I told them, but on how they decided to use it. Having no say in any of this I didn't really think about it.

I just wanted to keep my wits about me and stick to my story while maintaining self-respect. I knew that I was being watched. My guards had seen many people in my position and must have wondered how they would behave themselves in the same circumstances. They did not strike me as brainwashed thugs. How would I have reacted had they been more brutal? I don't know. I think I would have curled up into a mental ball. As things were I was talking rather freely.

Back in the room the masks came off and any feeling of fatigue soon vanished. The first voice was the aggressive one.

"You have given us an endless list of lies and evasion. Now I want to know what motivates you. Is it money? Blackmail? Ideology? Or just hatred?"

"Hatred?"

"Your friends in Israel hate us."

"I've never been in Israel."

"Your name is Lang. We believe that is your real name."

"Oh, yes."

"It is a Jewish name."

"What?"

"What is your mother's maiden name?"

I told him.

"What kind of name is that?"

"Scottish. Like Lang."

"Is she Jewish?"

"No. Listen, 'lang' is Scottish vernacular for long, meaning tall. It's a highland clan. One of them was the Archbishop of Canterbury, for God's sake."

"Which parent had you circumcised?"

Oh, God.

I explained that I was circumcised at age five or six. It happened on the dining room table where I was born. I thought there was some medical reason. The doctors came to our house and removed my tonsils and adenoids at the same time, which was a medical fad in those days. I was told I would get ice cream afterwards but never did. It was during the war or soon after it.

"What religion were your parents?"

"Scottish Presbyterian. But they weren't religious."

"They never took you to church?"

"Very seldom."

They were curious about this. Neither of my parents was religious? This would figure of course if one of them was a Jew and the other wasn't. Had my father's family converted or did they still practice Judaism?

Suddenly it struck me that there was a lot about my own family I didn't know. My mother was one of five sisters and two brothers. My father also belonged to a large family whom I almost never saw and about which I had heard very little. It now occurred to me that maybe these strangers were Jewish. I had always just assumed that my mother did not get on with them or something. Now I began to wonder.

Could it be true? Was I in fact a Jew? If so, what a time to find out.

"We think you are a Jew though not raised that way. Like your friend Lotz. Now you are in Egypt at a time when we are at war with Israel and you associate with another Jewish spy and a German who is working for Israel for money."

"Another one? Are you telling me MacKay is Jewish?"

"If that's his name. He could also have a Jewish mother. What do you know about his family?"

Jesus Christ, I thought. Drumnadrochit Castle. I said nothing.

126

They informed me that the person calling himself Martin MacKay was a spy working for Israel. Hans Goslich too. They were both well paid, like Wolfgang Lotz. What did I think of Lotz? they asked. Did I think he was a man of character? Did I think he was a patriot or a cheap opportunist?

All I could do was protest my innocence. The only money I had was what I was paid by the school. If there was a radio transmitter in my apartment I never saw it. They searched for aerials and I knew they had found none. Unless someone planted them. I remember the following exchange.

"We do not say you were transmitting from your apartment. We think you were keeping the equipment for those who had been using it."

"Then why did I talk about it? I showed the radio telephones to several friends who warned me to get rid of them. Would I do that if I were keeping them for spies?"

"To whom did you show the radio telephones?"

Again I caught myself. It was definitely my worst mistake so far. "I can't tell you that," I said. "You would go knocking on their door. But they are absolutely totally and completely innocent people. Like myself."

"Did you tell your girlfriend?"

"Actually, no, I did not tell her."

"Why not?"

"Because of her job. She might have to tell her boss. I didn't want that. You don't think she's a Jewish spy, do you?"

Staring at the lights, I had no way of telling their reaction. But in the end I was not unhappy with the way it had turned out. I think they saw that I had probably told Vermelle, but didn't want to implicate her. They did not press the point for now. And if they believed that, it would reflect positively on me and suggest that I was not a spy.

Unless for America. Or Britain.

CHAPTER THIRTY-TWO

Around this time they called another break. When I came back I sensed a lighter mood behind the lights, but did not relax. The first question took me by surprise.

"Have you ever been threatened or offered a bribe?"

"You mean in relation to Egypt?"

"Yes."

"No. Anyone who knows the first thing about me would not try that."

"They say that every man has his price."

"Really. So how much would it take to make me give up my child?"

"Do you have children? Legitimate or not?"

"No."

"Do you intend to marry and have children?"

"Probably not."

"Then why do you choose that example?"

"Because it's a good one.

"It is also interesting. You work with children." I nodded. "You once invited two young boys from the school to come with you into Cairo."

It wasn't hard to tell where this was going. "We went to the museum."

"And then you took them up to your apartment. Where you stayed for several hours."

"We had some snacks."

"And you made sexual advances."

"That's nonsense." But I felt the sweat. There had been several days since I was in the school. They could have been there questioning Ahmed and Mustapha. They would not have lied. Their influential fathers would not allow them to impugn their manhood even to please the state police. But under questioning they could have been persuaded to say that I had made suggestions which they didn't follow. Once again I felt trapped.

"Let's leave that for now. You have also entertained children from the street."

"What?"

"We have witnesses."

"Hold on." I had a vision of the always smiling face of the grinning doorman of my building. "There was a day when I was buying groceries outside. I dropped something and a kid on a bicycle said something that sounded like, "Helas salade!" which made me smile. I asked if he wanted to help me carry the stuff up to my flat and he agreed. He had a few words of English. How do they learn that? We brought the groceries upstairs. I would have given him some orange juice and chatted for a while. I've often wondered how the people in these houses live. He seemed a bright kid. I remember him quite well, wearing a blue and white striped galabiya. But I could see he was uncomfortable. He didn't want his friends outside thinking the wrong thing. So I gave him a twenty piaster piece and he ran off. My friendly doorman," I said acidly, "should be able to tell you he wasn't there long enough for anything to happen."

"And you went to the hammam. Just out of curiosity. Quite a pattern of behavior."

"What's this got to do with spying for Israel?"

"At this time we have not questioned any of those children," one of the balanced voices said. "But if you continue to be evasive and less than honest with us we shall do so."

"I take back something that I said before," I told them. "I have now been threatened. See where it gets you. I am innocent and have nothing to tell you but the truth."

For the next long stretch of the interrogation the focus of their questioning was on Martin MacKay and Hans Goslich. They wanted every scrap of information I could dig from my memory, including casual conversations, everything. Where and when had MacKay flown his plane and what had he said about it? My information was genuinely sparse, but I did recall his mentioning a trip to the Suez region where there was rumored to be a missile base. MacKay was not one to discuss politics, but I recalled him telling me that when Nasser nationalized the canal, the RAF had it under control in fifteen minutes before the Americans butted in. Our conversations, like most casual conversations, were not recorded in my memory. I finally

129

admitted that I thought his background sounded like a story for strangers and had not pressed him about it. It was mentioned when we first met and never repeated. Martin could be a bit of a conman. It had certainly not occurred to me that it was a cover story invented by a spy master. I knew very little about his job. He talked about a company based in Paris, but I wasn't much interested. The film they were making was some kind of technical thing. It involved Egyptian military campaigns but I had no idea how it related to his job. I knew he had a plane and a substantial bank account in Egypt, so he said, but no details on that either. He was always well dressed, usually in navy blue or black and had a nice car and I had never seen him drunk. He was definitely Scottish. I made no mention of the gem smuggling.

I knew even less about Hans Goslich and held back nothing. I had no doubt he was a spy.

It was only in the last part of the interrogation that they questioned me in detail about Vermelle and Yutaka Wada. Again I had nothing to hide, including her wariness of MacKay and Yutaka's comments about Lotz. Friends like Mooney, Picton, Ward-Green, and Mentakis were of only passing interest to my questioners, but still they made me repeat what I had told them many times. Same for colleagues at the school and Hindle-James, who seemed to be known to everyone in Cairo. As a general tactic they kept coming back to things. Martin MacKay is a friend of Wolfgang Lotz. I am a friend of Martin MacKay. What did they offer me? Money? Boys? Why had I infiltrated a woman who worked for the CIA? At some point I realized that I was tired. Very tired. But it was never long before a question came that put me back to full alert.

"Was it Wolfgang Lotz or his wife who was a big attraction to all the Egyptian friends they had?"

They were obviously trying to wear me down. But even on the edge of consciousness my brain is either on or off. Even when subjected to so-called truth drugs, I always know what I'm saying until I pass out. The repeated questions and harking back, however, let me know that I was far from being out of the woods.

130

CHAPTER THIRTY-THREE

During a silence behind the lights I closed my eyes. There was no drifting. I was wide awake. Suddenly the lights went off.

There were three men sitting there. One of them was Mr Aleesh in his dark suit. In the center was a bull-necked man I did not recognize who gazed at me assessingly. The third was a grey-suited man who might have been there on the morning of my arrest. It was the one in the center who spoke.

"We have decided that you are innocent. After some formalities, you will be released. Have you anything to say?"

I blew a long gust of air. "Thank God. Can I go back to my apartment?"

"Your apartment will be made ready. And your car is where you left it. Your keys and other possessions will be returned."

"You mean I am completely free? No trial? I can leave the country?"

"You will be released this afternoon. Tomorrow you can go back to teaching at the school. The headmaster has been informed."

"That's great. What are the formalities?"

"Just some paperwork. It will take an hour or two. Meantime, you have not eaten for a while. Would you like a meal?"

I have tried to recall if I were offered food while in the cell. If so I was in no mood to eat. Now I was being invited to specify a meal. I kept it feasible. I asked for fish and rice. I thought of requesting a bottle of Scotch but canceled the idea. I asked for coffee made in the American way to wash down the food. I would have preferred tea, but not the way they made it. In retrospect, I marvel at the alacrity with which my brain accepted the sudden and unexpected good news.

I now know that the man in the center was Salah Nasr, head of Egyptian security. I recall him as an aggressive

looking man with a trimmed mustache who was a powerful
and controversial figure in President Nasser's regime.
Following his lead, the atmosphere in the room relaxed and
became almost friendly. They asked me questions about
the countries I had visited. I recall that Mr Aleesh asked
me if Western women behave at home the way they do
when overseas in places like Egypt. I told him they behave
in exactly the same way. After this encouraging man-to-
man approach, they let me know that although they had
decided I was innocent that did not go for my friends
MacKay and Goslich. They believed that both were spies
working for Israel and Britain.

Hmm. They were spies but I was free to go?

The chat expanded to other people in the room. I
remember the stenographer telling me that he was a
wrestler and wondering if I had seen him on television. I
was almost beginning to believe that I was truly out of the
woods when they once again started asking questions
about Wolfgang Lotz.

"Is Lotz so in love with his wife do you think, or is it all a
big act?"

I told them I had no way of knowing.

"She's quite a woman, you must admit."

"I'm not sure I ever saw her."

"But getting their picture taken holding hands ... It's a
bit much, isn't it?"

"I don't know. I kind of like that sometimes."

"When you're sitting on a horse?"

During this the gun was still at my back. I assume I
was served the meal but do not remember eating it. After a
while I was told that everything was in order and I was
going home. The armed guard left and a couple of unarmed
men entered the room. I was blindfolded again and led
downstairs and out into a courtyard. I heard a car and
thought I was about to get into it. Instead I was turned
around and taken back inside. With no explanation I was
told to stand.

For a while I was aware of activity around me and the
voices of guards. Still blindfolded I wondered what was
going on. Without explanation I was then taken further
into the building and led back upstairs. When the blindfold

was removed I recognized a room in which I had been waiting earlier. Always the optimist, I had not given up hope of being released but wondered what the problem was.

As time went by I began to wonder if they really intended to let me go or if this was all a sham. From what I'd heard it would be typical of the psychological tactics which at that time I associated with brutal foreign regimes. The worry grew that even if they believed I was innocent they might keep me in detention to prevent me from communicating with people like MacKay and Goslich, who were now safely out of Egypt. Then it occurred to me that perhaps one or both of them had not managed to leave at all. I had seen Martin to the customs check. But they could have stopped him after that point and for all I knew he was being interrogated in the same building where I was now and saying God knows what about me. Lotz and his wife were certainly being questioned. The fact that they didn't know me from Adam didn't mean they weren't saying something. During this I heard gates and car doors and the voices of guards outside. I went to the window which overlooked the courtyard and saw another poor wretch, blindfolded and staggering between two men, being dragged into the building. I wondered if he were connected with me. Maybe I would have to wait until they had gone through the same routine or worse with him and maybe he would say something to make them change their minds about releasing me – if they had ever intended doing so in the first place.

At the time I estimated that I spent about two hours in that room. Unlike my time in the cell I made no effort to contact the guards who I'm sure were just outside the door. Deprived of meaningful resistance and with no way to predict the future, I saw no reason to do anything but hope. I did not pray. I just hoped that things would work out for me as they always had in the past and if they didn't, I would just have to deal with that when the time came.

The door opened and they were back in the room. Blindfolded again I was taken to an office occupied by the man I would come to know as Salah Nasr. My watch and keys and shoe laces were lying on his desk. A wallet in those days was a slip of leather that carried money, nothing else. Since having my pocket picked in Paris I did not carry one. A few banknotes that had been in my hip pocket were lying on the desk. I put the watch on my wrist and the laces in my pocket. He told me I would now be taken home. My apartment had been opened up. I have always had a mild case of Tourette's syndrome. In those days it was an eye tick which I know had been working overtime. He mentioned that they'd noticed this but that my personality was extremely stable. I had looked very guilty for a while, but in fact was not. We shook hands. All I wanted was to be allowed out of there. Now it really looked as though it would happen and it did.

That, however, was not the end of it.

CHAPTER THIRTY-FOUR

At this point I can replace memory with words written at the time. One of the many mysteries in my life is why I failed to make a permanent record of the events in Cairo while they were fresh in my mind. True it was a busy time and continued to be so. Also I probably assumed the details were permanently engraved – which is true to some extent but with plenty of exceptions when you try to recall details. I did write an account of the arrest and sent it to a British newspaper when I was back in London. But for reasons that I now understand it was not published and I have no record of it. The document I do have was kept by my parents and contains some details that would otherwise have been lost in the mists of time.

The letter reproduced below was received by my parents in Scotland on Tuesday the 13th of April, 1965. It was typed on airmail paper onboard a vessel called the Lydia as I crossed the Mediterranean to Greece. The account is focused mainly on what happened after the interrogation and gives some of the flavor of my last weeks in Cairo. At one point it can be seen that even then, with the events very recently behind me, there is some confusion over the passing of the days.

The following is word for word even to the punctuation of the eight page letter, which I found in my father's possessions when he died in 1999. I can well imagine how he and my mother read and reread it many times.

Dear Mother and Father,

Well out of Egyptian water and I can relax for the first time in three weeks... This is Wednesday, eight o'clock in the morning -- tourist lounge of an old tub called the Lydia. At about noon Thursday we should arrive in Piraeus, from where I shall drive (yes, I still have the Corsair) to Athens. I have friends in Athens and some good introductions from friends in Cairo, so I should not be short of a place to stay and have a

*chance of finding some sort of job quite soon... (I'd
better because I have no more than ten dollars to my
name... this is the maximum they let you carry out of
Egypt). Of course I have a very nice car and a
typewriter and record player with many records,
altogether worth over a hundred pounds... I can sell
these things (apart from the car) but I shall do so
only if absolutely forced.*

*Of course, you want an explanation of all this... I
hope you won't think I'm exaggerating when I give it.
I have been forcedly incommunicado on the subject...
almost completely incommunicado in fact.*

*My last letter I wrote on a Friday. I told you about
the things I received from this German. Well,
amongst these items I found a small radio-telephone
(illegal in Egypt) and a miniature tape recorder of
which the tape was no more than a fine nylon
thread. I noticed these things, but I thought little of
them. Goslich was a technical man and had a great
mass of electrical junk, amongst which these two
were not very conspicuous. But I mentioned them to
a few people and was warned that they were
dangerous things to have... I didn't pay much
attention...*

*I wrote to you on the Friday. On the Saturday
evening, I had a big dinner party in the new flat.
Sunday evening I drove the departing Jim Picton to
the airport and saw him off to Saigon (he escaped
the bombing, by the way). Back from the airport I
went to Maxim's bar and stayed there until about
four o'clock... The following day, Monday, was a
holiday...*

*Then I had been in bed for about one hour when I
was awakened by a tremendous battering on the
door. I staggered up and seconds later the flat was
full of the famous and much-feared, Gestapo-trained
Egyptian Central Intelligence... They ransacked the*

*flat, found the radio and tape recorder (I showed
them where these were) and, amongst Hans
Goslich's papers (which I hadn't even looked at) they
found code keys and transcripts, plans, documents
of a terrifyingly incriminating nature... Of course I
had no knowledge of these and said so. They did not
argue... I just had to get dressed and go with them.
   I was then taken down to the big black car, blindfolded and driven across Cairo for about half an
hour... horn tooting, gates clanging... then, still
blinded, I was led down stairs, along corridors and
into what felt like a cold room. The blind-fold was
taken off and I saw the three grey walls of a tiny
cell. They searched me thoroughly and took away all
my possessions. Then the door closed... I don't know
how long I was left there because they had taken my
watch, but it was a good few hours. Occasionally I
went to the window in the door of the cell and asked
what was going to happen – how long was I going to
be left there. The answer was always the same "We
don't know. It is an order," which I did not find very
comforting... At last the door was opened and I was
blind-folded again and led up some stairs, along
corridors, into a room and placed on a stool. The
blind-fold was whipped off and I was blinded by the
classical arc-lights and a voice said, "Now tell us
how you met Wolfgang Lotz." ...And I actually
laughed. Lotz is a spy they had just caught in Cairo –
a German working for the Israelis – I had seen him
on television and corrected an article on him for the
newspaper... Lotz was the talk of all Cairo at the
time. Of course I had never met him and said so.
They were puzzled at my laughing and disappointed
that their shock tactics hadn't worked and settled
down to an interrogation that lasted 14 hours. Later I
was offered food and drink and they became almost
friendly, telling me they had decided I was innocent
and that I would soon be taken home. (Before leaving
my flat they had closed up the shutters and cut off
the gas and water as though I was going to be away
for an indefinite spell.)...Then, after being more or*

less nice to me for a time, they gently started asking questions about Lotz again, putting me right back on guard.

Finally I was told that I was going home. The armed guard went away (I was at gunpoint during all this time) and was replaced by an unarmed one. I was blind-folded again and led down-stairs, out into the court-yard. I heard the car and thought that I was just about to get into it, when suddenly, I was turned around and taken back inside, told to stand. I stood like this for some time and was then led back upstairs to a room that I had been waiting in earlier. I was there for two more hours – plenty of time to wonder if they had changed their minds about letting me go – or if they had ever intended letting me go – this would be typical of their psychological tactics. I was very worried in case they would keep me in detention to prevent me from communicating with the two others, Martin MacKay and Hans Goslich, who were safely out of the country and whom the Egyptians would obviously like to get their hands on. Then it occurred to me that perhaps one or both of them had not managed to leave at all. I had seen Martin to the customs, but they could have stopped him after that point. I am still not absolutely certain that he got out... Anyway, while I was being detained I heard gates and car doors and voices outside. I went to the window and saw another poor wretch, blind-folded and staggering between two men, being led down the same stairs, presumably, as I had been led down earlier. I wondered if he was connected with me – if I would have to wait until they had gone through the same routine with him – perhaps he would say something that would make them change their minds about me. I had plenty to worry about during those two hours... Then I was taken to the office of the head of internal security, my things were returned to me and I was told that I had been found to be completely innocent. I was then finally taken home.

I went straight to the car and drove to Vermelle's place – but although it was late, she was not at home (I found later that when my servant had arrived at my flat the previous morning, there had been a security man waiting for her and he had scared her so badly that she had gone round to Vermelle's flat, crying and hysterical, and had succeeded in scaring Vermelle so badly that she had gone off to stay with a girl-friend). In the car I was tailed by a big black car. I then went into a snack bar which the journalists used and met Hugh Mooney, who wanted to know why I hadn't turned up for Jim's work. In this bar I was followed by no less than four security men. So they were convinced that I was absolutely innocent, were they.

Since that day I have been followed everywhere, on foot or in the car. My flat has been watched twenty-four hours a day and all my telephone calls have been tapped. Of course, I informed the Embassy and they advised me to leave Egypt immediately – if I could. The Intelligence chief had told me that I would have no trouble getting an exit visa if I wanted to leave – nor would I be obliged to leave – but assurances like this mean nothing in Egypt, nothing at all. So I resigned from the school and started the tremendously complicated machinery of leaving in such circumstances.

Of course I could write nothing of this in letters. In fact I did not even post any letters except to hurriedly sign off the one that I had previously written to you. I mentioned the incident only to a few close friends, who had instructions to report to the Embassy if I were missed for any complete day... However, I found an American who was passing through Cairo and was due to leave in a few hours and took the risk of telling him something of what had happened and asking him to contact MacKay in London and warn him on no account to come back to Egypt. Even

*if he is a spy, I have no desire to see him fall into the
hands of these people.*

*The Consul General, Charles Palmer, wanted me to
get on a plane and go straight to London as soon as I
could get a visa. But I wouldn't agree. I wanted to
travel by boat to Athens and take MacKay's car with
me, and the things I could carry in the car... Palmer
got furious at this, saying that it would be impossibly
complicated and would just give them a chance to
hold me up. He was very worried about the
Egyptians making something political out of it
(innocence or guilt being neither here nor there in this
case – just a scape-goat British spy to embarrass our
government for political reasons. On paper, you see,
by missing out a few things, they would have a very
good case against me). Palmer kept pointing out that,
just at this time, the Egyptians have reason not to
want to annoy our government, but that this was, he
assured me, liable to change, perhaps in a matter of
weeks. But I held fast. I was going to be leaving
without money and without job, having lost, in the
first place, my four hundred pounds sterling summer
pay, and I wanted at least to have the car, which
MacKay will get back when I am good and ready
and not before... During the interrogation I did
everything (and not without risk) to protect him and
put all blame and suspicion onto the German... Some
of the answers I chose with some care, in spite of the
insistence and shock tactics. (They told me at the
end that they thought I was very stable, in spite of
my eye-tick, which was working overtime and which
they had immediately noticed.)*

*For a time it looked as though Palmer was right
about complications. The school wouldn't give me the
letter releasing me from contract which I needed for
the exit visa. They said that they would have to
contact their lawyers and the central intelligence. (In
fact the intelligence people phoned the school and
assured the headmaster of my innocence and that*

there was no need for me to go. I said that if they put this in writing and lodged it with the British, I would stay. This, of course, was refused... The incident made everyone even more concerned than before.) Also the travel agency told me that I would have to pay for my passage in sterling, which meant that my Egyptian money was useless and I would have the problem of getting sterling without telling people about what had happened. (The Embassy would have paid my passage to London, but not to Greece, for some reason.) Also I did not have the carnet for the car and the only thing I knew about the man who had it was that his name was Habib, which is like Smith in Cairo. Martin had meant to give me the name and address of this man before he left, but in fact he forgot and of course I couldn't write to him. Also, Cooks told me that the authorization I had from Martin was not enough to let me take the car out of the country. All these things were at their most hopeless one day when I went out to Heliopolis to search for the address I wanted in Martin's flat (of which I had the key, but which I had been forbidden to visit by the Embassy). I found that I couldn't get in, even though I had both keys. So I got hold of the landlord – very frightened looking man when he saw me – who told me that the servant had latched the front door. I pointed out that I had the key to the back door as well and couldn't get in there either. He informed me, smiling sickly, that the servant had latched that one also. "Then how is he going to get in?" I said. "Come to that, how did he get out?" The wretched man had no answer and I knew that the flat had been sealed by the police. It was at this lowest possible ebb that I visited the family in Heliopolis who were looking after Martin's dog, which was ultimately in my charge. I told them roughly what had happened and said that I might soon take the dog away. They were so frightened that they insisted that I take the poor bloody animal immediately – they had their children to think of and they wanted nothing whatever to do with the

*business, not even to keep the dog another day...
This attitude may seem incredible to anyone living in
a country like Britain, but to anyone who knows the
score in modern Egypt, and the horror of Nasser's
secret police, it is understandable. All the same, I
thought it was a bit weak for an Englishman... I was
left with this little dog on top of all my other worries,
in a flat four stories up in the centre of Cairo, which I
hardly visited, I was so busy every day and my
servant scared away.*

*At this point I used the special 'phone number they
had given me and told me to use if I were in any
trouble. I took the pretext of a suitcase which they
had taken and not returned and mentioned at the
same time the trouble I was having. I was told that a
car would come to take me to the same building to
meet once again with one of the most powerful men
in the country.*

*I went straight to the Embassy and reported this to
Palmer, who literally tore his hair. He said that they
had instructions from London to put on as much
pressure as possible to get the documents from the
school and an exit visa and to put me on a 'plane for
London as soon as this was done. I asked when the
pressure was going to start. He said the date was
fixed for two days later. I said I had a feeling that
the (Egyptian) Intelligence would help me to leave as
happily and unsuspicious as possible, so that I
would tell MacKay that the situation was not so bad
and perhaps encourage him to come back for his
aeroplane and the five thousand pounds he has in
the bank there... Either that or they did not intend
letting me go at all, in which case neither Embassy
pressure or anything else would help. Palmer
thought I might be right, but still thought I should let
them handle it. I thought about it and finally decided
to use my own judgment in a situation which was
totally uncertain and which I knew more about than
anybody. They had the experience, but not so much*

of this sort of thing, because this sort of thing does
not happen every day, and I was the only one who
had ever met the people in question or had any kind
of direct contact with them. So I decided to go to the
rendezvous and made arrangements to contact the
Embassy before a certain time... The Egyptian police
chief listened to my tale of woe, asked a few more
questions (directed towards the question of Martin's
return) and told me not to worry. I had been warned
that involving myself with Martin's car might make
them suspicious, so I raised the point specifically and
asked if it would make them suspicious. He said no,
it would not.

Next day, before the Embassy pressure had started,
the school came through with the letters and I went
straight to the government offices and obtained an
exit visa in the record time of 15 minutes. Under
normal circumstances, this process takes at least
two days. Next day, the travel agency (who were
clearly expecting a visit which should have been
unexpected) suddenly decided that I could pay for
my passage to Greece in local currency and that my
authorization for the car was sufficient. At the same
time, I found the man Habib who told me that the
carnet was in Alexandria and to come back the
following day. Now tomorrow usually means never in
Egypt, but when I went back he had the carnet – but
it was out of date – this was why he had had it, to
get it renewed, but with Martin out of the country he
had quite typically not bothered to do anything at all.
I was told that this made everything quite useless,
that it was 100% impossible to export a car on an out
of date carnet. But to get a new one is a business of
several weeks, so I decided to rely on the powers
behind sight.

Thus I bought tickets for this boat and came down to
Alexandria on Monday evening, accompanied by a
man from the Embassy to see that I had actually got
on the boat and not been stopped after passing

*through customs, where an ordinary person would
have had to leave me... I had been instructed in all
seriousness not to go into bars or night clubs, the
fear being that something might be slipped into a
drink and my falsely accused of breaking the peace
or something when I came to and thus detained.
(This very James Bond warning came from the
British Consul.) ... The worry at this stage was that
the police had been helping me simply to make me
relaxed and unsuspicious so that I would perhaps do
something interesting during the last few days – but
with no intention of letting me go out. The instruction
about not going into bars I completely ignored and
finally arrived at the Alexandrian docks early
yesterday (Monday) morning. For my own part
everything went well, but the car they would simply
not pass on the out of date carnet. The Embassy man
tried very hard but could do nothing. He finally told
me that I'd have to leave the car, which the Embassy
would try to ship after me. But I wouldn't give up – I
wanted to see the Director General. I was in the act
of looking for him when a porter brought a message
from the Director General asking if I would go to him.
He knew my name, spoke very pleasantly, wrote
something in Arabic on the carnet and said they
were very sorry for all the trouble and suffering I had
been caused.*

*So that was the end. The car was put on the ship
with all the luggage in the boot and as I said, we
passed out of Egyptian water long ago.*
  *Quite a little adventure story, isn't it? It was pretty
hellish at the time of course – the worry and strain
were considerable and right up to the last minute. All
the same, I don't think I suffered as much as some
people would have done – at least I wasn't so scared
as to get on a plane to London without any of my
things.*

*Tomorrow (Thursday) I am arriving in Piraeus about
noon and will drive down to Athens, where I will*

immediately contact a Greek family the son of which I knew very well in Cairo and who conveniently went home two weeks ago – he went back for good after living in Cairo for many years. He has spent most of his life in Egypt and will be looking for a job same as me. He belongs to a well known family apparently and has the best possible contacts, of which I shall also have the benefit... I suppose they will put me up at first until I have some money coming in (Jon knows all about what happened and, understanding the full implications of such a situation in Egypt, is fully sympathetic... In addition I have an introduction from Hindle-James (the old man who hired me a servant) to Sir Robert Maxwell, who knows about Egypt and who, I am told, will do everything to help.

So I think I should be all right in Athens. (The main thing, of course, is just being out of Egypt.) On this boat I have met a very pleasant man from Oxford, who is also going to Athens (on holiday) who will benefit from my car (it's a half hour drive to Athens from the port) and who will see that I am not stuck for a few pounds on the boat or at customs.
  Now, when it is all over, I am not at all sorry that this has happened. It makes a fascinating experience in retrospect and I am very much looking forward to Athens. I've lost a lot of money, but I've gained a beautiful car for some indefinite period. So I'm very happy now... Tired, but quite pleased.

I'll post this from Athens along with a hand-written post-card. Make no mistake about it – I really am there.

Love,

Norman.

P.S. The dog I gave away to a boy from the school. He belongs to a big family, so the dog will never be alone, which is a good thing.

Also, I was so financially stable in Egypt that I was able to handle this emergency without borrowing anything. In fact I had pounds left over at the end which I couldn't take with me, which I spent on clothing before I left Alex.

N.

CHAPTER THIRTY-FIVE

The month of March 1965 happened to be a busy time in Egypt. Not only had the secret police arrested an important spy who was making the news worldwide, but there were other major events in the air.

On March 18th (three days after my arrest) while Lotz and his wife were still being interrogated, the deposed King Farouk, whom President Nasser had to see as a potential threat if the British or Americans ever decided to reinstate him, died of cardiac arrest after eating a large meal in a restaurant in Rome. As in the case of other sudden deaths of prominent Egyptians, there were theories about how this might have happened. According to sources close to him, the controversial and much feared head of Egyptian intelligence, Salah Nasr, was unusually preoccupied and nervous during this period. One of these sources, a woman called Etmad Khorschid, who wrote a best-selling book after his death in 1988, reports that Nasr was in her house that evening and told her, "Farouk will die tonight." It has been suggested that Farouk was poisoned using aconitine, a drug that has been said to have been used before and since by Egyptian intelligence. According to some reports, Egyptian agents were in the restaurant that night and Farouk's female companion, a woman called Anna Maria, abruptly left the restaurant as soon as he started to complain of feeling ill and has not been seen since by news media. There is another reason why the time period was a busy one. On March 25, Nasser himself was sworn in for his second term as Egypt's president.

In retrospect I have wondered to what extent these background events might have affected the way the intelligence chiefs dealt with me. Maybe they were overloaded and just too busy to spend a lot of time with a prisoner they couldn't quite figure out. I wanted to believe they had perceived my innocence in spite of the evidence against me. But one had to wonder if they were simply letting me run meantime in the hope of learning more. The

key question – Would they let me leave the country? –
remained unanswered till I rose that morning on the good
ship Lydia, took my typewriter from the trunk of the car
which was very surprisingly still in my possession, and
wrote the letter to my parents.

The letter gives a fair idea of the flurry and stress of
those last weeks in Egypt. Reading it truly takes me back.
At the same time it leaves unsaid a number of things, some
of which I knew at the time, others not until later.

After meeting Mooney and finding Vermelle's flat empty
on the first night, I went back to my apartment and got
some solid sleep. The next day, driving to the British
Embassy, I knew immediately that I was being followed.

The British Consul, Charles Palmer was a tall, balding
man who sat behind a large desk in front of a mantelpiece
draped in flags in a large, sparsely furnished office. He
listened to my story, asked some questions and there may
have been some formalities which I don't recall. What I do
recall is his reaction. It was a sticky situation, he said.
There was the potential here for embarrassment for the
British government and a lot worse than that for me. From
my description he identified the senior interrogator as
Salah Nasr, whose name I had either not heard or not
taken note of until then. I was in trouble, Palmer told me.
They had sent a bigger team to bring me in than when
arresting Lotz. But not to worry. There was a lot going on
at this time. Nasser and his pals had a few things to think
about. If we played our cards right and acted quickly, he
was hopeful that they could have me back in Britain before
the Egyptians had figured out what to do with me.

I'm not sure what I said at this point. I was concerned
about Vermelle and probably mentioned the car, but was
still winding down from what I had been through. I agreed
about resigning from the school and leaving the country. In
spite of all the assurances I had been given, there could be
no feeling of safety while still on Egyptian soil.

It was probably later the same day that I drove to the
school. My escort saw me into the parking lot and parked
outside. I was almost surprised that they didn't follow me
in. I met with the headmaster and apologized for having to
leave them in the lurch. I had truly enjoyed teaching at the

school and found the young people disciplined and interested. I also spoke to some of the teachers and remember that there was a representative of the British Council who happened to be visiting that day. Let me repeat what I have said before that if this school was a place where hatred and religious intolerance were preached – as is the connotation of the word madrassa in the present day in the United States – I saw no evidence of this in either the students or the teaching staff. They all seemed sorry to see me go and I could see it in their eyes that they wondered about my immediate future. The assurances of the security chiefs persuaded no one to whom I spoke, young or older.

That afternoon I called Vermelle and found her at home. She told me that when Fatima went to my apartment on Monday morning she had been met by a security man who had told her I was gone for good. I assured her that I was back in my apartment and did not feel immediately threatened. She was embarrassed that she had been afraid to be alone even in the embassy-connected building and invited me to come over for supper.

One of the specific memories I have is of the brown eyes of the slightly more mature woman as she watched my face and listened to my story. Americans tend to have a lot of common sense. They are by no means more intelligent or clever than the British, but they are more street-smart and less likely to take you at face value. I cannot say just what she was thinking, but I think she felt that I was over optimistic about my chances, especially in regard to the car. She cooked a chicken, which was one of several in her freezer. This reminded us of the terrible story of the woman who had died trying to get one for her family. I have positive memories of that night and several others that followed it. I think I spent as much time in Vermelle's apartment as in my own in those days. She was one of the small number of friends I told of my arrest and one of the even smaller number not afraid to be in my company after it.

In this context I want to say that another person who showed what I call courage was my Japanese friend, Yutaka Wada. I told him the story and mentioned that some of my American and British friends were afraid to be in my company knowing that I was being watched by Nasser's secret police. His words were, "I am not afraid." One can say that his diplomatic position made him feel secure, but I think it is also a question of character. Hindle-James was another stalwart. He might have felt confident because of his connections, but so did Wolfgang Lotz. The elderly Englishman told me to come by any time, and before I left I gave him cutlery and other items including money to pass on to my servant, Fatima, who had fled while I owed her wages.

As the days went by, the difficulties mounted. As mentioned in the letter the school refused to release me from my contract. This was on the strength of a call from Internal Security telling the headmaster that I had no reason for breaking it and in the Egyptian system this meant that I could not obtain an exit visa to leave the country. Also I lacked the documentation to export the car and everyone assured me that this was something I would never receive. Cars were like gold in Egypt. Some government official surely had his eye on it. The British wanted me to leave by air. They would facilitate that and even pay for it – but to London, not jaunting around risky parts of Europe. I don't know who pressured the travel agency to tell me I needed hard currency to pay for a boat passage. Maybe that was the reality, maybe not. Then I found myself in possession of MacKay's dog, a quietly disturbed puppy. The little guy was not neurotic, but was subdued for a young dog.

They were busy and frustrating days. "Against *bureaucracy* the gods themselves struggle in vain." I had Scotch, courtesy of Yutaka, and chicken thanks to Vermelle. And an official escort everywhere I went. The Consul, Charles Palmer, was an experienced diplomat. I respected him and had nothing against him as a person. But I had to stick to my guns more than once when he seemed about to leap over his desk at me. The Egyptians could keep a thing like this on ice for years, he told me. I had to get out while the going was good, which would be hard enough even with the influence of the British government behind me. The sooner the better, I said, but

not without the car. If they didn't like that they were going
have to put up with me till they let me take the car. I was
damned if I would leave it for some bureaucrat.

At some point I sent a telegram to the address I had for
Martin in London. I told him I was leaving Egypt for
personal reasons, implying a family emergency. I said
nothing about the car or any other developments, but
added the rider "Will try transport dog." This of course was
far from my intention. It was designed to make him think.
Not knowing what news he might have heard, I was
warning him not to return to Egypt. (I had little doubt that
on reading the telegram people like Mr Aleesh would guess
what I was doing but calculated that they would let the
telegram go through and in fact they did.)

As mentioned in the letter home I visited Martin's house.
The fact that it had been secured by the police did not
surprise me, but my God, the fear of people for their own
government! At the same time let me say that in my view
the Egyptian people, like the people of most nations in a
time of stress, basically respected their government and
believed that they were doing what was necessary in a
hostile world. I have lived in ten different countries and can
safely say that I have never met a single person who was
not a patriot. Everyone is, young and old, those who
criticize their governments and those who don't. As sure as
mothers love their children, every country is full of
patriots.

They say that trouble comes in fours, or even fives and
sixes. Trying to get out of Egypt on my own terms seemed
impossible. But in spite of frantic warnings from the
Consulate and the advice of friends, including the gentle
warnings of Vermelle, I did not believe that my
uncooperative actions, even if they extended my stay in the
country, increased my chances of finding myself back in
Tura prison. I alone had met the men who would make this
decision and felt that I knew as well as anyone the facts of
how I stood. For whatever it was worth, I did not feel that I
was resented as an individual by any of those I had
encountered. I think there were those who wondered if I
were innocent or a tough professional. I could almost hear
their voices: "This Englishman is either very smart or

stupider than we think possible." But I did not feel hated.
It was, however, a tense period. I spent long nighttime
hours wondering what would happen if I were rearrested
and subjected to physical torture.

I visited the school again and was scolded by the
headmaster. He accused me of taking fright unnecessarily
and breaking my contract. I pointed out that he was not
the one who had been arrested in the night and thrown
into a cell. I recall that he was being visited that day by the
owner of a private school in Europe who gave me his card
to write to if I were looking for a job. I thanked him, though
at that time, I have to say I saw my future as a kind of
distant, far-off dream. Job hunting was a practicality.
Maybe I would be doing it again someday when I was back
in England safe and sound. I thought of this rather in the
way I imagine people thinking of the promise of a paradise
hereafter, when no longer burdened by this mortal coil.

During all this time my telephone was tapped. I could
almost hear them breathing as they listened. I remember
the day when I used the special number they had given
me. I have an image of myself in the flat above Midan el
Tahrir talking to a case officer at the other end telling him
that some property had not been returned to me. I
complained that I was an innocent party being obstructed
at every turn while trying to leave Egypt with my legal
possessions. I was told that a car would pick me up.

I did not wait for the car. I drove to the consulate and
spoke to Charles Palmer who almost fainted when he heard
that I was going to meet with the GIS, the General
Intelligence Service. He strongly advised me not to do that.
I could say a wrong word and it would be all over. The
British government was working hard to get the documents
I needed from the school. After that, if it all worked out, I
would be on the next plane to London. I thanked him
sincerely for all their work on my behalf.

When I left the consulate I saw the gentleman in the
ubiquitous black car parked off the road looking back at
me from the open driver's door. I have no doubt that they
knew very well that I knew I was being followed, if for no
other reason than because I mentioned it in almost every

telephone conversation. I drove back to my flat and a car was there to take me to the meeting.

As one of those strange things that one encounters when recalling events like this I do not recall the venue of the meeting. As things happen one is focused on essentials like a person's face, not his name or the location in Cairo. It was probably in Tura prison, in the same room where we met earlier, that the man I now knew to be the head of Nasser's secret police repeated his assurances. As mentioned in the letter he assured me that they were not blocking my exit from Egypt. Nor did trying to take MacKay's car affect this one way or the other. He did not say that they would help me take the car, just that they would not use that or anything else I had done to date as a reason to detain me.

Charles Palmer tore his hair. Vermelle shed a quiet tear. Hugh Mooney spoke to me with wrinkled brow. Phillip Ward-Green told me I was off my rocker.

After visiting Salah Nasr that day, I decided on a nostalgic visit to Maxim's Bar.

CHAPTER THIRTY-SIX

My companion that night was a young Englishman whose name I remember well enough; let's call him Gordon. He was a graduate of one of the better universities and was in Egypt as part of a traveling vacation before starting on a career in finance or something of the sort in London. He was in the country on a visitor's visa, not working, and was staying with one of the English guys; it could have been Hugh Mooney.

Gordon was an inch or so under six feet, elegantly built, with a handsome and young-looking English face. Not in the least effeminate, but having attended public school he had to know what it was to be admired. I found him intelligent company. How we met that night I don't recall. Probably we met in one of the snack bars and decided on a beer. It was a time when I was not given to spending a lot of time alone in my flat.

I remember the young doorman found me distracted and said so when he saw me come in that night. Didn't I want to hear my phrase of the day? I told him he was a lousy language teacher and gave him a good tip in advance before noticing Gordon being detained in the doorway behind me.

The other player in the incident was a black American whose name and background I totally forget; let's call him George. He was an undisguised homosexual of the type who seem to think of almost nothing else. I had nothing against George and didn't mind talking to him when we met, though he was not one of our group.

George and some others were leaving the bar as we came in. While talking to the little doorman I looked back and noted something that did not need explanation. He detained Gordon with a hand on his waist as he spoke in his ear. With his arms at his sides and not looking at George the younger man spoke quietly and moved on, clearly rejecting the invitation to leave with George. I could tell it was not a first time encounter but made no comment as we went to the bar and ordered beers.

I don't know how long I packed his ear about what was on my mind. I told him about the arrest and the fact that the whole of Cairo seemed to be conspired against me. The British wanted me out without the car and other possessions. The Egyptians didn't want me to leave at all and were making it difficult at every turn. The British position was illogical. If I were in so much jeopardy the Egyptians weren't going to let me out whether I rushed to the airport or not. Even the travel agency was making things difficult. I remember giving my back to a dark-suited Egyptian who sat next to me and warning Gordon to say nothing of consequence within earshot of the barman. He was interested enough, but seemed distracted. We drank some beers until I became oppressed by the sense of secret police around me and we left the bar. As we walked along Kasr el Nil I realized that my companion had something on his mind and finally it all came out.

He had gone to a party the other night with some of George's gang, he told me. I scarcely had to hear the rest. They'd ended up having sex all over the apartment and Gordon was not proud of what had happened. It was not private either, he said ruefully and saw me wince. Now he supposed there was nothing for it but to catch the next plane out of there.

Whether or not he was asking my opinion I immediately gave it. If he were ready to leave Cairo that was one thing, I said. If it were due to embarrassment over this incident, it was totally unnecessary. To George's crowd it was not a landmark event. To the rest of us even less so. It would not be the talk of the town, even to those who heard of it. I wouldn't mention it to anyone. So he had stayed over at one of George's parties. So what? Was he a different person? It was simply no big thing.

For the next hour we walked the streets. We talked about places to travel in the Middle East and I repeated my reassurances about his brush with homosexuality. Sometimes we had to find out what we weren't. Whatever I said, it must have been the right thing for once. Gordon did not flee the country and seemed to have forgotten the whole incident next time I saw him.

155

It was late when I went back to the bar on my own. Careful of the barman and just about everybody else in the shoulder-to-shoulder environment I reviewed my own decision to flee the country, which in a sense was against my instincts. There are times when taking flight invites trouble.

One of my well-remembered dogs was a large boxer. Sometimes he would escape unleashed and unintentionally terrorize the neighborhood for a while. Named Randy (after Randolph Turpin, an English boxer who unexpectedly defeated Sugar Ray Robinson and was world middleweight champion for a while) he was not a vicious dog with people, not at all, but had his way of getting what he wanted. One day he took a parcel of fish from the shopping bag of a lady. When her husband tried to get it back, the dog growled at him. When the man backed off and began to run the dog went after him. Later that night the man came to my parents' house and complained about the dog. He said it had chased him all the way to his front door and he was lucky to escape. A brash teenager, I apologized for the incident but pointed out that if my dog had wanted to catch the man it would have done so very quickly. It lollopped after him because he ran from it. Humans often do the same, but with worse intentions.

As I walked home, for once I did not see them in the almost empty streets. I was taking an expected route and was pretty sure that there were eyes on me, but from doorways and maybe windows. I was not alone. If rearrested, there would be no warning. When I entered the building I was glad the friendly doorman was not in sight. I was in no mood for his grin. I went upstairs and was met by MacKay's waggly young dog. He at least was glad to see me. I poured a glass of Scotch and spoke to it for a while, before checking that the doors were locked and latched and going thoughtfully to bed.

CHAPTER THIRTY-SEVEN

The first thing I recall of what happened next was opening my eyes and knowing there was someone in the apartment. I'm a light sleeper. If you even pause at the doorway of my room I'll waken. I threw back the covers and froze. There were footsteps in the hallway.

This time no banging on the door. They were inside before I knew it. I recognized the bull-necked figure of Salah Nasr as he walked into my room with several others, who ignored me until I spoke and was pushed back from the doorway. I reached for a bed lamp but my wrist was gripped.

"What's going on?" I asked. "I thought you told me I was innocent."

"You think we are fools?" he said. "Lie on the bed."

"Do you mind if I get dressed?" As usual I was wearing a pajama bottom and no top.

For an answer I was pushed back hard onto the bed. In the darkness I found my hands and feet restrained. I made no attempt to fight them. How do you fight a group of men who enter your house at night and work together against you? They had switched on no lights. Shielded flashlights only. This gave the intrusion an unreal, furtive air, attracting no attention from outside, which I'm sure was the intent. I said nothing, did nothing, no real thoughts.

There were several of them in the room. They seemed to be setting up equipment of some kind, their voices very quiet. I was on my back, head half- raised against a pillow – not for comfort, but to give him access to my face – as he pulled up a chair.

"All right, now tell us when you first met Wolfgang Lotz."

The room seemed unnaturally dark. Even at night there was usually an ambient glow on the window blinds. Looking past the man who questioned me I saw a shadow. Not a shadow, rather a suggestion of light against which I thought I saw the shadow of a head. The questioner sitting close to me was Salah Nasr.

"I do not believe I ever met Lotz."

"We think you're lying."

"It's the truth."

"You are being very foolish." Now I saw the scalpel. It came to within an inch of my right eye and stopped. I stared upwards.

"For whom do you work?"

"I work for the Madrasa el Nasr."

"Be intelligent. That is your cover. I'll ask again. For whom do you work?"

"I am a teacher. That's my only –"

"Liar!" The point moved fractionally and if anything came closer. I felt that if I blinked it would cut the eyelid. "You should know better than to lie to me. One more chance before I puncture this eye . . . . For which intelligence agency do you work?" There was a long sigh. "Very well."

I heard my voice as though it came from another room.

"I was recruited by MI6 in London. But I don't know much about the organization. I was briefed for a specific mission."

"What is your mission?"

"To locate missile bases in the Suez region."

"Why Suez?"

"It is within easy striking distance of Tel Aviv."

The scalpel stayed poised. "Is he telling the truth?" he asked someone.

From the bottom of my eye I saw the suggestion of a head that seemed to be bent over equipment of some kind. It moved negatively. "No. It's all lies."

The knife flipped. A sharp pain went to the center of my brain. I felt warm fluid on my cheek.

Bastard!

Someone in the next room started screaming. For a moment I thought it must be Tura prison. Some poor bastard couldn't take it.

At that time I had heard the term "hog-tied" but did not know what it meant. It means your wrists are bound to your ankles, like a pig being taken to the slaughter. I was on my back and scarcely able to move except my eyes. I blinked. The blood cleared. There was vision.

"I decided not to blind you yet. I have a soft heart. But not for long. Before this night is over you will tell me who you work for, why they sent you here, what you learned, and what you have reported. Until you do, this night will seem like all eternity. For which country do you work?"

It wasn't Tura. We were in my apartment. So that was their strategy. No torture in the prison. When they left here there would be no witnesses. Neither from the residents of the building nor anyone else. My wounds would be called self-inflicted. I had been released from Tura unharmed. Even if I were found dead, I was just a foreigner who had committed suicide.

"There's nothing I can say. I can't even lie to you. I have no good lies and have told you all I know."

"Start the drill," he said.

It sounded like a lawn mower being started. The sound came from beneath another shadowed head. The questioner's voice was now hard against my ear. Above the din, I heard the intake of breath before he spoke.

"When did you first meet Lotz? Was it in Paris, with his Jewish wife and child? Or in London?"

"No . . . . No..."

"Or through the one who calls himself MacKay?"

"I met MacKay in Cairo as I told you. To my knowledge I have not met Lotz. For God's sake, you must know I'm not lying!"

The whine of the electric drill came closer. It eclipsed thought. My mouth was jammed open. The one in the next room started up again.

We are going to drill your teeth.

Self-inflicted wounds? They didn't give a damn. They could do anything they liked.

"Who is your contact in Maxim's Bar?"

I tried to answer, but the drill was in my mouth.

"Is it the Englishman you met tonight?"

I signaled and the drill moved back a fraction.

"Gordon? He's as innocent as I am."

"The woman?"

"What woman?"

The sound of the drill rose to fever pitch.

"What woman?"

159

"She is in the next room."

It took a moment. The face of the man behind the drill came into view. It was a bearded face, with eyes like coal, sweat in the creases of the skin.

I used my legs and broke the cords that tied my ankles to my wrists. Suddenly my arms were free and there was no one to restrain me. But try as I might I could not move. The commands went from my brain but my body would not move. I could see myself lying there, teeth clenched, trying desperately to move my limbs which would not obey. I was my own enemy. And this was not a dream. It was real. It was not a dream…

When I wakened I was on the bed. The window was there with the lights of Cairo behind it. For a moment I had no idea who or what age or where I was. Then the room came back, the feel of the room, my thoughts.

"Vermelle?" I called her name. "Vermelle?"

The little dog was there. When I said his name he tried to lick my face.

"Bed, Wolfy. Good boy. Go."

The feeling of the dream ebbed slowly. It was going to be a laster, I could tell. Like a dream I'd had in Paris that I was dying of poison in a metro train the walls of which were vivid red and green. I was dying in that colored train as we traveled to an unknown destination. I knew this dream would last. (More than forty years later I can still see the face behind the dentist's drill, which resembles no one I consciously remember seeing.)

I got up and walked through the rooms of the apartment. I was intact, no cuts or bruises. I checked all the rooms. Everything was as it should be.

But what did that mean? How should things be at this juncture of my life? I asked myself, as images from the dream still flashed in my mind.

CHAPTER THIRTY-EIGHT

The day after the meeting with Salah Nasr things began to turn around.

First the school came through with the letters I needed to apply for an exit visa. I went straight to a building in central Cairo (I believe it was the Mogama building but there are other official buildings) and requested an audience with the Minister of the Interior. The administration in Egypt was still small in those days. They knew who I was and were sympathetic. I remember the interior of a large building with impressive stairways of wood and marble. While waiting I asked how I should address the minister and was told that Your Excellency would be appropriate. I was not kept waiting long. I had waited longer in a doctor's office in my hometown.

The office I was shown into was huge. An elderly man in diplomatic garb with a fringe of grey around his bald head and with glasses on his nose sat at a desk in the center. I addressed him as Your Excellency and he thanked me, which I felt was a polite reaction to a foreigner whom he knew was not used to showing such respect to government officials.

I told my tale of woe for the second time in two days. He was sympathetic and without further ado granted the authorization I needed to leave the country.

My next stop was the travel agency. I flourished my exit visa and found that there was suddenly no problem with leaving by boat and paying in Egyptian currency. All I needed was the carnet for the car and I could take that too.

The next day I tracked down the man called Habib who I think was employed by MacKay in some capacity but who was not under suspicion of any kind. He was probably a police informant like many private citizens in those days. He had the all-important carnet, but it was out of date. As I explained in the letter home he had neglected to renew it.

Well, that changed things, the travel agency told me. There was no way I could take the car until the carnet was renewed.

161

Back in the British Consulate, I requested their help in renewing the carnet. I was told that this was something the Egyptians had to do and it would take weeks and I would be insane to wait for that. I had the exit visa now and there was still a chance that they could get me out. They would escort me home right now and I could collect my things and they would try to get me on a plane this afternoon. When I shook my head Mr Palmer was not complimentary. I was being unbelievably reckless, he said. A lot of people had spent a lot of time on my behalf. If I had no concern for myself, could I give a thought to the interests of my country? I told him I had plenty of concern for myself and my country, but did not see the relevance to the latter. As for the interests of Harold Wilson's government, excuse me but I didn't even vote for him. I then thanked him for all their hard work on my behalf and asked if it extended to helping me get out of Egypt with the car.

When leaving the Consulate I touched the horn in the avenue that led down from the embassy buildings in case the driver of the black car was asleep. Back in the travel agency I purchased tickets for the car and myself on a boat leaving Alexandria in a few days' time. They told me I was good to go, but trying to take the car was a waste of money without the carnet. They accepted payment in Egyptian currency.

During the last few days in Cairo I found a home for the dog. This made a substantial difference to my frame of mind. Egyptians are not dog lovers. They have much the same attitude to canines as they do to pigs, which they don't eat. But I found a family with children who wanted the dog and did not seek MacKay's blessing in giving it away.

Leaving Vermelle was a different matter. I have no wish to dwell on that except to say that it was an uncertain and traumatic time. I was either going off into the wilds of Greece or back to Tura prison. That would not be known until I was either out of Egypt, probably for all time, or still in Cairo for the foreseeable future. We spoke optimistically. I would try to let her know when I was safely home. I gave her my address in Scotland and asked her to get news to my parents if the worst happened. The authorities would do this of course, but a personal touch would surely help if it came to that. We wished each other the best in our future lives, and I recall the emotion of parting more than the details of what we said to try and reassure each other.

I said goodbye to Hindle-James and his retinue of youngsters. If there was any harm being done to anyone in that situation I did not see it. He just liked them better than most adults and preferred their company to an empty house. My servant, Fatima, was still terrified to be seen with me but I tried to compensate her by leaving things with Hindle-James. Before I left he gave me an envelope with a handwritten introduction to Sir Robert Maxwell, a British media tycoon who had recently been elected to the House of Commons and who would be sympathetic, Hindle-James assured me, to my problems in Egypt.

I had a boozy farewell with Mooney and Picton and Ward-Green. We exchanged addresses and talked vaguely of possibly keeping in touch. If I got out, my next stop was Athens where Jon Mentakis was expecting me. There were British and American schools in the region. Such places were often looking for qualified teachers of maths and science. I would be okay. Especially if I had the car.

James Picton, who was back from Saigon, was able to help me in another way. All the cash I had was in Egyptian currency which had no value outside of Egypt. I could turn this into dollars on the black market but would not be allowed to take it out of the country. Being paid in dollars Jim had to convert some money every month for living expenses. I gave him most of what I had and the address of my parents in Scotland. The deal was that he would send a check to them till the money was used up. I can report that he did this, though I never saw the man again.

In the letter home I say that a man from the embassy accompanied me on the trip to Alexandria. In fact I think he met me there after I had driven the desert road from Cairo. If the Egyptians wanted to detain me they did not have to stage a disappearance in the desert, though that was a genuine threat. While driving on that lonely road I saw some gentlemen on camels who watched me from the sand dunes. I remember thinking (as I had been warned) that this was no time to have a breakdown or even a flat tire. I remember scanning the road for signs of anything that might damage the tires, and wondering how fast I could go after a blowout.

The embassy man was an educated Englishman a few years older than myself whose main function was to ensure that I was allowed to board the boat. I met him as planned on the Monday afternoon. He was pleasant and promised to do his best to get the car on board before the ship left next morning. We ate dinner and I went to my hotel where we had arranged to meet in the morning. How he spent the night I don't know, but I did not spend the evening sitting in my hotel.

Though I had been warned not to go to bars in those last days, I had never been in Alexandria and wanted to nose around. What else in a strange city when you've only got one night? The Egyptians had no way of knowing in advance where I would go and I was now pretty skilled at taking note of people who came in after me and keeping an eye on them. I ordered Stella beer and watched them open each bottle. Yes, I was followed, but not by anyone who tried to distract me or communicate with the bar staff. I was probably safer than I would have been in the hotel.

In one bar I bought a couple of drinks for a lady who was there ahead of me who spoke French. We talked about life in the poor parts of the city and how people got by. I could see her wondering what I might be looking for and what it would be if not herself. I told her I was leaving in the morning on a boat for Greece and she said she was envious of my life.

The next day started off with no surprises. The embassy man did his best but met with total failure in regards to the car. The carnet was out of date and that was it. But not to give up, he said, surprising me. The embassy would take charge of the vehicle and attempt to get the carnet renewed and then ship it to me in Greece or wherever I wanted to receive it. He asked how that suited me. All he had to do now was make sure that I was on the ship when it sailed.

I said that all sounded fine but that I wanted to speak to the director general of customs. By this time I knew that he was the person in charge of the docks. The embassy man was amused at first. But when I started speaking to customs officials, demanding to be taken to the office of the director general, he began to show the same symptoms as Charles Palmer. I was going to get myself arrested, he said. I was playing right into their hands. I was finally beginning to lose hope when a porter approached me on the docks. He said that if I would come with him, he would take me to the office of the director general.

The office was the typical large room with shaded blinds and a desk in the center. A large, Farouk-like figure in a dark suit sat at the desk wearing dark glasses. He asked me for the out-of-date carnet. As he scribbled on it he said they were sorry for all my troubles. My car would be put on board the ship and I would have no trouble at the other end when I showed the carnet, on which he had written in Arabic.

I thanked the customs chief and went outside. I saw my car with all the luggage it contained being lifted onto the ship.

The embassy man shook my hand and was pretty well speechless. I remember that he shook his head a lot as we spent the last hour before sailing. During that time there was an end piece to the story that I did not mention in my letter home.

In leaving Egypt I was allowed to carry out only the equivalent of five Egyptian pounds, about eleven dollars in hard currency. One of the things I had been warned about was not to try and smuggle more. In stores around the docks I bought some things but still had money that was literally worthless outside the country – no one would accept it or exchange it. The embassy man and I were having a coffee when a street urchin approached and held up five fingers saying, "Khamsa, khamsa," that is "Five, five," by which he meant five piasters (pennies) for a ball-point pen he was carrying. He was pretty surprised when I gave him thirty pounds. I should say that Egyptian money in those days was worth more than ten times what it is now and people earned much less. Thirty pounds was probably more than the boy's father earned in a year. He did not speak English. I tried to tell him in French that he had enough to buy not one, but two of the little machines that roast peanuts that are sold on street corners by entrepreneurs. I don't know if he heard a word. He ran off delirious. I have always wondered what happened to that youngster, if it made his fortune or cost him his life.

CHAPTER THIRTY-NINE

The boat trip passed in a blur. I guess I was winding down after weeks of stress. I do not recall writing the letter or meeting the "pleasant man from Oxford" who in retrospect was probably a representative of British intelligence. I have a vague memory of staring at Crete and surrounding islands as we came closer to the Greek mainland. None at all of docking and driving the Englishman into Athens. The Mentakis family graciously hosted me in their home in Tenedou Street. They were extremely kind and hospitable and I very soon found a job at the American school of Athens, where most of my colleagues were English. I have memories of those months but none very relevant to this memoir.

My memories of Athens and the coastal regions of Piraeus are mostly culinary. I loved the tavernas, with the spreads of butter beans and octopus and fried fish and the metal mugs of retsina wine. Also the atmosphere where families dined on solid tables close to each other and spoke to strangers across the sawdust covered floors. I have images of that and seafood meals at the coastal cafes and above all of the Acropolis, which we visited one day. I am not a great sight-seer as a rule, but the ancient pillars of the Parthenon are in my mind. You don't need to know much about the history of classical Greece to feel it in your bones as you walk amongst these stones.

By the time the school was closing for summer break I was in contact with Martin MacKay and had agreed to meet him in Athens. Our plan was to drive the car to Geneva where he would sell it and I would get a plane home.

I met Martin at Athens Airport and remember the look of annoyance on his face when he did not immediately spot me in the crowd. This is a natural reaction, but it told me that he and possibly others to whom he had spoken were not confident that I would keep the rendezvous. He told me he'd been contacted by Whitehall, the home of Scotland Yard in London, who informed him that I had been arrested. I did not challenge him when he said that this was the first he'd heard of it. In addition to my telegram he had been warned not to return to Egypt and indicated that he had no intention of doing so.

To me it's not surprising that we picked up like old friends. He was a bit fed up about some damage to his car, which had been in a fender-bender but was glad to see it again, and I had more to think about than whether he was spying for Israel or anybody else. Martin was a person with no great interest in intellectual things. He was not a seeker after truth or meaning and I cannot imagine he had deep ideological convictions, but I can see him as an adventure-seeking spy. If we had gone to school together we would not have been close friends. He would not have been on the rugby team or outstanding academically. But as compatriots meeting in Cairo we hit it off, and whatever his other motives might have been was of no great concern to me. We talked about his dog and his servant and his worried landlord and what had happened to me with the fucking Egyptians. He had no special girlfriend to my knowledge, but had a lot of interest in Vermelle and whether I planned to meet her out of Egypt. We talked about the trip through Italy which we planned to make into a bit of a vacation. I must have asked him what he thought about Goslich and the incriminating junk he'd left with me but got no clear answer.

There is one exchange that I recall. When I told him about the kid in Alexandria wanting five piasters and ending up with a small fortune, Martin's comment was, "He probably meant five pounds." I was astonished. Five pounds for a ball point pen? He shrugged and had no more interest in the conversation.

As we drove north to the town on the Adriatic from which we would take a ferry to Brindisi, Martin was at the wheel of the car and at one point asked sharply, "Where's the power?" I pointed out that we were on a steep incline, not uncommon in these parts, which was why he had no acceleration. If a spy, he didn't seem to have much operational training.

While crossing Italy I recall that we stopped at a village called Potenza in the mountains on the way to Rome. There was a wedding celebration going on and the landlord of the local inn had no great interest in his foreign guests, but we managed to get some grilled meat and pasta and red wine. I have no recollection of our conversation, but there was something about the simple meal that made it memorable. If Martin talked about himself I don't remember it. I don't think he had attended university but I can't even be sure of that.

We visited Rome and Naples before driving up to Switzerland. I remember enjoying the food and the atmosphere. Sitting at dusk on a verandah outside our hotel in Naples, I remember remarking that the Italians really know how to live. I guess I was watching the people in the street at the time. I remember his quick glance beneath a wrinkled brow as he followed my eyes to see what I was looking at, which was a group of students. He did not challenge the statement but I noticed that it meant nothing to him one way or the other.

To this day I can't be sure if Martin MacKay was a spy or just what he claimed to be – and I'm not even very clear as to what that was. The official evidence said he was a spy. But the same is true of me. And if his lack of interest in pressing me on the subject indicates that he knew more than I did, what about my lack of interest in pressing him? True I had other things on my mind at the time. I was beginning to feel the bottom as the waves got shorter and I drew close to home after what seemed like a long and traumatic absence.

We reached Geneva where he had buyer for the car. Was that the full reason for his trip or had he been assigned to assess whether I was going to be problem? I do recall his interest in the letter to Sir Robert Maxwell. How did Hindle-James know Maxwell? I had no idea. I'm sure I mentioned that I would probably write up the experience and send it to the *Times* or the *Guardian* but have no recollection of his answer.

Whatever happened to his plane in Egypt and the money he was said to have there I have no idea. I must have asked and in retrospect I guess he was good at evading questions. We shook hands. I remember the smile on his black-shadowed face as we said goodbye. What made him tick I still don't know. It was the last time I saw him. I took a plane to Heathrow and drank a few pints of bitter while waiting for the connection to Glasgow. I had to smile at seeing Englishmen again with their noses in newspapers and trays with tea and breakfast on their knees as they waited for their business flights. An American in sneakers took in the scene as he sat with his wife and children on their trip to Europe. I was home.

CHAPTER FORTY

During that visit home I was surprised and delighted one day to answer the telephone and find myself talking to Vermelle. She was calling from the States but sounded as though she could be next door, telling me that she just wanted to know that I had made it home safely and asking how I was. Partly due to my surprise we didn't say much more. I was instinctively guarded on the telephone (and still am to this day) and we were literally worlds apart. At that time I had no plans to visit the States or ever be back in Egypt. I thanked her again for her support in Cairo and we spoke warmly to each other and that is the last time we spoke.

In London I found my old car, the 1947 MG, still parked in Finchley Gardens where I'd left it at the side of the road near the apartment where I'd lived. The black canvas top of the red two-seater was covered in leaves and the tires were low but after some coaxing and charging of the battery a friend and I got it going. So I had wheels again in the old banger that you drove almost lying down, behind a bonnet like the prow of a ship stretching out ahead of you.

Not in a regular teaching position I had no summer pay. I found a job in a remand home for juvenile delinquents called Stamford House in Shepherd's Bush. It was an interesting few months. I learned that most juvenile delinquents are basically no different than other kids and remember some of them and their teachers quite well. The discipline was better than in secondary moderns I have taught in.

I wrote up my story and sent it to one of the major newspapers. The only reply was a brief "No, thank you," which I now know was inevitable given the sensitivity of the material. I did not attempt to contact Sir Robert Maxwell. By that time (summer, 1965) I knew that Sir Robert was a prominent supporter of Israel and was rumored to work for the Mossad, and something told me that he would not be encouraged to speak to me. Rightly or wrongly I chose not to contact Sir Robert.

CHAPTER FORTY-ONE

In August 1965 Wolfgang Lotz and his wife were found guilty of spying for Israel and sentenced to life imprisonment and three years, respectively. Reading news reports from the safety of England I observed that the trial was open and very much a propaganda issue, which would explain the careful treatment of prisoners, including myself. Years later Lotz claimed that his wife had died from coercion she suffered, but there was no physical evidence of this and it was not mentioned during the trial. It wasn't until two years later that we learned the full significance of it all.

Wolfgang Lotz died in 1993, twenty years after his wife, Waltraud. Since then there has been a good deal written about his role in arming Israeli intelligence with information that led to the military success of what is now called the Six Day War. In that strike Israel destroyed the air power of not only Egypt, but Syria, Jordan, and Iraq all in the morning and early afternoon of June 5, 1967.

As an example of what has been written, the following is from a 2010 article in the Jewish Virtual Library. (*)

Egyptian pilots woke up to the sounds of their planes exploding on the ground that morning...

Israel's tremendous military success came not only as a result of the high level of training, expertise and courage of her pilots and soldiers, but also as a result of accurate intelligence. As Samuel Katz writes; "It is safe to assume that in no time in the history of modern warfare has a nation been equipped with such an intimate portrait of the enemy's disposition, deployment, abilities and inabilities as was the IDF... on the morning of June 5, 1967." King Hussein of Jordan later said; "Their pilots knew exactly what to expect ... their pilots had a complete catalogue of the most minute details of each of the thirty-two Arab air bases, what objectives to strike, where and when and how. We had nothing like that." Israel's Intelligence had been so attentive they knew the exact timing of Egyptian patrols and their air routes. Air Force commander Moti Hod told chief of staff Yitzhak Rabin on June 4: "For two past weeks we have been keeping watch on the precise movements of the Egyptian air force ... at first light they take off on patrol, staying up for an hour. Then they return to base and go off for breakfast. Between seven and eight everything is dead, and 7:45 in the morning is the ideal time for us." That was the exact time that the Israeli Air Force struck.

The groundwork for the successful penetration of the Egyptian and Syrian militaries was laid by Wolfgang Lotz and Eli Cohen, but many other spies, both Israelis and Arabs – and sometimes European or American non-Jews – also worked on behalf of Israel.

There were "many other spies". In 1965 we knew that very well. What we did not know was the extent to which their work would be significant two years later. Lotz and his wife were caught and went to prison, but hardly for life as it turned out. In 1967 they were released in a prisoner exchange and returned to Israel. Lotz's personal account of these years can be found in his book *The Champagne Spy,* published by St Martin's Press in 1972. In this he makes no mention of the Six Day War, but gives indirect indication of how he was caught. Israeli intelligence doesn't like to admit it, but Lotz himself remarks in a footnote that the Egyptians were helped by the technology "of another country" (Russia) in tracking his transmissions. Details of this technology are described in my first published book, *The Last Ramadan,* a novel based on my experience in Cairo.

Years later, when the First Gulf War was launched in 1991, the issue was still sensitive. Even now, long after Lotz's death in his native Germany, the book is still closed.

In the summer of 2010 I finally decided to write this nonfictional account of what happened in Cairo in 1965.

One of my first acts was to write to the British Home Office asking for information which I hoped would help jog my memory. Specifically, I asked if they would release what they had on file concerning my arrest. The answer was a polite letter telling me that they were not at liberty to release that information. If I wished to take the matter further I had to write to the Secret Intelligence Service (SIS).

I wrote to the SIS and in due course received a polite rejoinder telling me that in the interests of national security there was no information that could be released to me even under the Freedom of Information Act, which I had not attempted to invoke. A similar though less formal telephone inquiry to the Egyptian Embassy in Washington, DC was met with a promise to get back to me. No one ever did.

I've made no serious attempt to track any of the people mentioned in this memoir. Some will have died, but some are surely still alive, and I apologize if some names have slipped my memory. The Englishman I have called Phillip Ward-Green, for example, is a person I remember very well, but his name totally escapes me. (Sorry, friend, if you are still alive and ever read this.)

* "Israeli Intelligence in the 1967 War" by Doron Geller.

CHAPTER FORTY-TWO

This memoir is not an autobiography and I have no intention of trying to make it one. But given the length of time that has passed since the events described, a few personal details might be in order.

The Cairo incident left me still not ready for graduate school. After a couple of years in London and Canada, during which I read mathematics and did some teaching, I finally went to Tulane University in New Orleans and graduated with a Ph.D. in mathematics in 1971. By this time Lotz and Waltraud had been released in a prisoner exchange and returned to Israel, where she died in 1973. Lotz never returned to his first wife and child, but traveled the world and wrote a couple of books.

After a year of post doctoral research, I went to South Africa and taught at the University of Cape Town where I met my wife (Jewish as it happens) Cheryl Herschbaum. Before long we gravitated to New Orleans (where people say you can't leave the city till you've found yourself) where we ran a restaurant and I taught at the University of New Orleans for a while till our son was born. After that I switched from the academic world to industry and soon joined the defense industry (anti-submarine warfare and missile defense).

In spite of now having a child and a demanding job, or maybe because of it, I finally got a couple of novels published in 1991 and 1993. Both are in the spy genre; one set in Cairo (*) and the other in apartheid South Africa. By this time we were living in New Jersey and I had started on an ambitious third novel set in the defense industry in Cold War days.

Then tragedy. In 1994, when our son was ten, Cheryl lost her battle with breast cancer at the age of forty-five.

I could say that the hiatus in my writing career was due to personal tragedy and the demands of being a single parent. There's truth in that, but there is also the fact that world events, including United States foreign policy in the wake of the Cold War, had gradually changed my political orientation to the point where my spies and villains didn't always fit the popular mold. I produced manuscripts which publishers praised for their authenticity and interest, but were not prepared to launch in their submitted form.

As already noted, this memoir was written before the current events in Egypt – even before the collapse of the regime in Tunisia. I have strong feelings about these events in the Middle East. They will reverberate not only in the Arab world. But I have told my story as I've always seen it, as a glimpse of how things were at the end of Nasser's days, before the Sadat and Mubarek regimes took over in Egypt.

(*) *The Last Ramadan* is set in Cairo in the summer of 1970, just before President Nasser mysteriously woke up dead one morning. In the story an assassin is sent to Cairo to get rid of Nasser in the only way possible.

EPILOGUE

I

WHAT NEXT?

April, 2011

In recent months we have observed the momentous changes taking place in the Middle East. After many decades of Western-supported authoritarian rule, during which we were constantly being warned that these countries were likely to become dangerous theocracies where the people have no interest in democracy, we now know the opposite. In countries like Tunisia, Egypt, Saudi Arabia, Yemen, Bahrain, Jordan, and Iraq, not to mention Libya, Syria, and Iran, there is a large class of educated younger people, as well as a suppressed middle class, who want to see an end to the corruption, the wealth-stealing by the wealthy, and, more fundamentally, a closing of the Western umbrella that has supported these regimes and promoted our interests at the expense of the people of the countries. They want to see all this come to an end in the only way such things can come to an end: through control by the many not the few – in other words, democracy.

During my time in Egypt President Nasser was on record as saying that Egypt was not ready for democracy. That was not my opinion then and it is not my opinion now. In those days the city of Cairo had a population of rich and poor living essentially side by side. Now, after decades of our protection, the wealthy are super-wealthy and live in gated compounds outside of the city, the poor are just as poor and the educated young are unemployed. Certainly there is a large group of less educated people who will be swayed by what they hear and see on television and will make decisions based on that and what seems to immediately concern them. In what way does this differ from any other democracy, not excluding those in Europe and the United States? The consensus of opinion across the country will nonetheless be better for the country as a whole than the will of a self-interested dictatorship.

The question remains, of course, will it be better for the rest of us? The answer to that might be debatable. There are certainly those who do not relish the prospect of having to be more realistic in the way we deal with key countries in the Middle East. In past decades we have dealt with selected leaders and ignored the people. Until we saw the masses in Tahrir Square, most Americans didn't even know such people existed in these countries. So where does that leave us?

During the Egyptian crisis we saw the leadership of the United States apparently divided on the issue. This is surprising only because the division was deep enough that it became public knowledge. In my view, it is one of the most important things that has happened in my lifetime: that in spite of the conventional wisdom, the leadership of the United States ended up on the right side of that issue, coming as it did at a critical point, after the collapse of the regime in Tunisia and before other dominos began to fall. We could have taken the wrong side of that and stored up nothing but trouble for the future.

The warning voices talked about Islamic Fascism. The Fundamentalists would go on a rampage against Israel and the rest of the world and the only way to counter that was to keep them down by force. It is one of the sad facts of life that a population is easily kept down by force – for a while. A regime hires an army and police force who have their jobs and families to think of. They will do what they are told by their political bosses who tell them they are protecting their country. If small groups like Al Qaeda decide to protest violently this is taken as proof that the repression is justified and so it goes on. But repression cannot last forever. The time will come as surely as a child grows – and in today's world that happens quickly.

There are those who point out that the Palestinians elected Hamas. Surely that is proof that such people are not ready for democracy. The response of the United States and Israel was typical. They ignored the people and decided which leaders to recognize. That's been the pattern, but no longer in today's world. What we see in Egypt is an amazingly peaceful demonstration by people demanding an end to repression and corruption. If nothing else the courage and determination they displayed should be enough to tell us that it's time to listen. The demand is for democracy. Not for Sharia law or anything resembling it even in their own country. In Nasser's day there was nothing of the sort and there won't be now. Certainly there are voices for it, as there are voices for almost anything when things are in a state of flux. But that is not the public will either then or now. Nor, surprisingly, has there been much in the way of anti-American sentiment so far – because we did the right thing for once.

There are those who tell us that President Obama started all the "trouble" in the Middle East by talking to the Muslim world and reassuring a quarter of the world's population that we are not waging a war against Islam. Those are people who would keep their foot on the pressure cooker till it blows them aside. Can anyone believe that what happened in Tunisia is due to President Obama and not the incendiary situation there? But you will hear it said by the same people who tell us that the current president is dangerous for Israel. If I lived in Israel, I would be breathing a sigh of relief that so much has happened peacefully.

Religious devotion is a fact of life not only in the Arab world. It exists everywhere and gets used by politicians. Deeply religious people can feel deeply about other issues and connecting lines should not be drawn. In modern Egypt the chances of an extremist theocracy coming to power are negligible so long as reason reigns. Unless of course we enable it as we did in Iran.

Not that anyone expects plain sailing. Even in Egypt, where things have happened comparatively peacefully so far, the years of suppression have given rise to a situation where there is no democratic tradition. In some of the other countries, where the leadership is refusing to give up power and religious divisions—although superficial—are perceived as being deep, democracy and coexistence might take longer. But I find reason to be optimistic. There was a day when Roman Catholics and Protestants were at each other's throats in Europe. It seems pretty silly now. In the modern day, with world news and mass communication, the differences between Sunni and Shiite Muslims will vanish quickly I believe, unless stirred up by the enemies of both.

When I first came to the United States in 1968 there was a new thing in the air called Women's Liberation. There was no shortage of people, mostly men, who were absolutely against it. Family life would go to hell and the cost of everything would escalate to accommodate two income households. Without two incomes no one would be able to survive. Some of the arguments made sense but there was one big truth that simply could not be ignored. Whether for better or for worse, it had to come.

After what we have seen in Egypt, those who argue against democracy in the region, however they phrase it, are clinging to failed logic. They are also denying the inevitable. To use a catch phrase, but in no sense lightly, if you like Iran, you would just love the Middle East and Muslim world that could emerge if we repeat the errors of the past.

II

A WORD ON TORTURE

I have been asked what if anything I learned from an experience which, if not unique, is hopefully still rare in our troubled world. If learning implies the acquisition of something worth passing on to others, I'm not sure about that. I certainly don't claim special insight into the psychology of torture or interrogation. But the experience does heighten one's awareness of an issue that is relevant and sadly still controversial in our world today.

We can all imagine being tortured. I think most of us have done so and it's not a pleasant thought. What we can't know for sure is how we would react. Most people say they would say anything to make it stop. We would certainly want to make it stop. But surely it matters what's at stake. At bottom what we want to know is whether torture is a valid or perhaps even necessary means of interrogation?

I was not tortured. But I was faced with it and remember very well how my mind was working at the time. I was prepared to lie. The reasons don't matter much. In the event, I was able to maintain these lies through persistent interrogation. Would I have maintained them against torture? If not, is that an argument in favor of torture? An interesting question is whether serious torture can ever be resisted.

In a psychological spy novel which I hope to complete some day (*The Electric Spy*) the main character asks, "Can you torture a woman to betray her child?" Ask an intelligent woman this question and she'll probably say she doesn't know. In the story his answer is you can't, so don't demean yourself by trying. This of course is fiction. But it's fiction written after at least being close to the situation and the more I think about it, the more I think it's probably true. If you can coerce a man to betray his country it's only because that doesn't mean as much. Try making him betray his child.

One hears stories that the Germans tortured French resistance people to betray the locations of resistance families including their own wives and children during World War II. I frankly doubt these tales. They may have tricked some people and intimidated children. But I think it's a rare patriot who would go out to fight the invader and then deliver his or her loved ones to escape the pain, however extreme. According to the cat-stroking Klaus Barbie, the Gestapo chief in Vichy France, "They all talk in the end." That may be true, but what do they say?

In his book, *Torture and Democracy*, published by Princeton University Press, Professor Darius Rejali addresses the same horrific case of mass torturing. He claims that in France, as in other countries, the Gestapo learned more from informers and collaborators than by interrogating resistance fighters. The following extract comes from a section headed "Stories from the Resistance" in Chapter 22.

"As one would expect, the devolutionary cycle led the Gestapo to rely ever more heavily on torture. The cases discussed subsequently are the known ones. Perhaps there are more. Resistance stories are selective. However, overall, these stories confirm what one might expect from a study of torture elsewhere. What is surprising is how difficult it is to find specific cases where torture produced information that was not known by other means. In a war that produced countless thousands, or even millions of brutal interrogations, this is a poor track record. And in many cases, the voluntary betrayal is hard to parse out from the coerced.

"Those who were tortured or who knew the Gestapo's work, were less pliable than those who, due to their own unique psychological dispositions, merely feared the Gestapo by reputation and looked to their arrest as a plausible scenario in which to betray others. Those who resisted often surprised themselves; it was unpredictable who would break or not break under torture. Some broke because a particular torture, unbeknownst to the Gestapo, invoked a childhood fear, yet others changed under torture."

There are always those who break, or appear to break. But the value of what they say is still an open question. It is certainly true that the majority of people arrested by the Gestapo were not resistance fighters. Most were "suspects" arrested in random sweeps. Rejali cites the case of a resistance member called Raymond Basset who was seriously tortured. Basset reported that the dentist's chair torture to which he was subjected was so excruciating that "*had they started to question me at that instant, there was nothing I would not have told them.*" That is what he said afterwards. But in the event anger overcame pain and he told them nothing. According to Rejali: "*Hardcore members did not normally break... Gestapo agents tortured leaders of the German, French, Belgian, Dutch and Polish Resistance. Among these only one* (whom he names) *broke under torture.*"

There was, however, plenty of disinformation. After interrogating the resistance leader Carl Goerdler, the Gestapo arrested 7,000 people, executed nearly 5,000 of them, and sent the rest to camps. But: "*Despite Goerdler's supposed information, after six months of investigation, the Gestapo still had nothing like precise knowledge of the resistance movement.*"

It might be surmised that Goerdler had no qualms about implicating compatriots who were not active in fighting the invader. The morality of this aside, what does it tell us about the effectiveness of torture?

The record books are full of cases where political prisoners under torture have made statements that were false, but welcome to the torturers. To quote just one example, the Libyan Al Qaeda member Ibn al Sheikh, under coercion in Tura prison in Cairo, where he was sent after being arrested in Pakistan shortly after 9/11, declared that Saddam Hussein had ties with Al Qaeda and was planning to supply them with weapons of mass destruction. Whether his interrogators believed this or not, their political bosses made use of it. Al Sheikh later died or was killed in prison in Libya.

This of course was "information" that was easy to give. The same could not be said of whatever information was obtained from Mohammad Zawahri, brother of the second in command of Al Qaeda, who at time of writing is still at large. Whether he knew anything or not, the younger

Zawahri spent ten years in Tura before being released in March of 2011 after the collapse of the Mubarek regime.

The ongoing question is to what extent torture is effective. Some proponents say that serious torture cannot be resisted. To me this is like saying that everybody has his price. If statistics were available, one could discuss the matter scientifically. For reasons ranging from national security to official reluctance there are no statistics, only rival claims and counter claims.

Rejali makes the interesting point that there are those who break, not under torture but because of the fear of it. Childhood fears and so-called truth drugs aside, it could be argued that there would be no such fear if torture were not there as a threat. Is this a sufficient argument for the use of torture?

A brief story about drugs. Undergoing anesthetic for a procedure, I remember the sharp pain in my hand. Doctors said it would soon pass and knowing my profession, asked me questions about the Aegis weapons system. They told me later they were trying an experiment. I remember everything I said until the moment I passed out while answering their questions with questions. I don't believe a skilled interrogator would have gotten more out of me.

Truth drugs might work on those who don't want to be tortured. Not otherwise. I would put childhood fears in the same category.

In this discussion we are not concerned with people who would break and cooperate at the mere threat of torture. Such a person is unlikely to have important information. He either knows that you already know everything he has to say, or is a bystander who should not have been arrested in the first place.

What can we say about the effects of torture when captured by a vicious enemy? Would a Marine tell you how to ambush his comrades? Would a terrorist who was ready to give his life to hit back at you give you information to foil his plot? You might say no harm in trying. The famous ticking bomb scenario (we'll come back to that). But to what level? Waterboarding into ice cold water is no fun. Nor is being beaten to a pulp. Would the Marine give in to

that? Would the terrorist? What then? The dentist's chair?
Genital mutilation?

Waltraud Lotz claimed that she was left lying in cold
water till she would speak. That's more than mild coercion
(according to reports she later died from the effects of it).
The claim is that she said nothing to incriminate her
husband and I can believe that. I also think we can see
both sides of it: the Egyptians wanting information about
people who were undoubtedly a threat to their country and
a woman determined to protect her loved one. Remember
that from the Egyptian point of view she was a known
Mossad agent living with a Mossad agent. There was every
reason to suppose she would know others. She didn't know
it, but her husband was telling them everything he knew.
They had reason to believe she might know more. Should
they have gone further when she didn't talk? How does our
imagination deal with that one?

A word on objectivity. There are those who think it is
unpatriotic to see any side of a war-time issue except our
own. When our national interests are considered to be at
stake, they will frown on anything that can be called
"encouraging the enemy". On a personal level, I can
understand the point of view. I might shield a friend or
loved one from the law. And although I am against the
death penalty—that does not mean there are no
circumstances in which I would personally carry it out. I
just don't want the State doing it. When it comes to
assessing the policies of a government, however, whether it
is our government or someone else's, there can be no
double standard. We can't say that it's all right for us to
torture the bad guys to protect freedom and democracy but
wrong for them to capture and detain our people. I might
be a hypocrite, but I don't want my government to act like
one.

In adopting a policy or strategy there are always pros
and cons. If there were a course of action that was always
right and never wrong there would be no discussion. Even
without meaningful statistics we have to try and look at
likelihoods and consider what is acceptable as national
policy.

At this time in the United States there is a school of thought which says that the Geneva Convention and rules of war are out of date and should be rewritten. The current rules do not cover people who "have no address" and are not controlled by a "legitimate" government they tell us. The same voices typically tell us that they abhor torture, but since it can be so effective (they often cite the Gestapo torturing of French resistance fighters) and since "we are going to use it anyway" they want it made legal. Specifically, they want a process set up whereby intelligence chiefs can apply for a torture warrant similar to a search warrant or a warrant for arrest.

The argument presented to justify this is the famous ticking bomb scenario. Suppose we have a prisoner who knows the location of a weapon of mass destruction set to go off in a couple of hours in New York Harbor. According to some there is *no* president who would *not* authorize torture in such a case and therefore we should 'fess up and establish a process that would create a paper trail and accountability. Torture should be authorized but only at the highest level. Which all sounds very reasonable until you stop and think.

Outside of television fiction, the ticking bomb scenario has not arisen in the fifty or so years since it was first imagined, nor is it likely to do so. I won't waste words on that. Assuming that the torture proponents are not speaking literally and are really talking about any emergency that is highly dangerous and possibly preventable, then what we have is the thin end of an undefined wedge. There is also the question of what kind of coercion we are endorsing.

For obvious reasons, the torture currently carried out by modern democracies is designed to leave no marks. Hence the popularity of electric shocks and waterboarding. But let's go with the hypothetical scenario. Given a possibly preventable situation with the imminent threat of massive loss of life and a convenient prisoner who might know how to stop it, is the president going to authorize waterboarding?

What then? Raymond Basset "almost" talked in the dentist's chair. Maybe if they'd cut off his genitals as well as drilling out his teeth he would have spilled the beans and told them everything.

By no means am I trying to make light of the problems we face in today's world. But nor can I take seriously this juvenile argument and it doesn't end there. I have seen in print (not by anyone mentioned in this book) that we should not hesitate to torture the wife and children of such a prisoner. The mind boggles at the breed of hardened enemy this would create worldwide.

But to answer the persistent "What if?" suppose Jack Bauer came to life and it all happened just like that and we have the prisoner sitting on a chair under a light bulb. What should we do?

At this point I have to mention something that caught my eye because of its succinct accuracy. In contrast to statements by more than one public figure applauding the fictional Jack Bauer for pointing a knife at the prisoner's eye (reminiscent of a dream I had decades ago) there was a response to a CNN interview on the subject that hit the nail on the head. Referring to the literal ticking bomb scenario, the blogger said, "In that case we've already lost." How true. But for the sake of argument, let's continue with the "What if?"

If I were Jack Bauer I would walk into the room and say, "For God's sake you're going to kill a million people. Not politicians or CIA or military personnel, just ordinary people. I know you hate our government. But this is not going to touch any of that. On the contrary, it's going to enable those who would hit back a hundred fold, which is what will happen in your country if this bomb goes off. So for God's sake tell us where it is."

To those who smile at the naivety of this I would say two things. One, it is the only form of interrogation that has ever really worked. And two, there is nothing in the proposal to make torture lawful in my country that makes me smile even derisively. And for whatever reasons, the majority of military and intelligence professionals agree with me on this one.

So let's forget torture warrants and the ticking bomb. What about the view that terrorists are an unscrupulous

enemy and if we learn something now and then by
torturing them why not do it?

When I was captured, I came from a country which at
that time did not use torture – not counting what might
have happened between soldiers in the field. Knowing this
gave me inner strength, but there's something I feel is even
more important. Although I cursed them at the time, in the
end I have no complaint about the behavior of my captors.
They had evidence. They had every reason to believe I was
spying against their country and were taking action that
was not inappropriate – some of it a bit harsh, but nothing
much different than I would expect of my own people. All
right, I was lucky. We still don't know whether it was luck
or good judgment or a calculation on their part that I was
released, but I was released promptly and unharmed.

A brief story on that. I was talking recently to a Special
Forces member who has worked with the Israeli Mossad.
He said, "Yeah, teaching is a common cover. But if your
cover was broken, why did they decide to run you?" I get
his point. To this day I'm not sure if my own mother fully
believed that I was innocent.

Well, I was. And I clearly remember those journeys with
the blindfold on. They knew very well that I knew very well
that it could end very differently at any moment, and if it
had ...

I have no trouble completing that hypothetical. To begin
with, the existence of the threat did not make me blab. I
lied to protect people that I hardly even knew. If tortured
and released, I would probably not have run to Tel Aviv
and offered to work for Israel, but only because I had other
things to do. I can promise this, however: I would never,
as long as I lived, have had an objective word to say about
Egypt or the Arab world. In my mind they would have been
the enemy from then on.

Now take the case of a young man arrested in
Afghanistan or Pakistan who ends up being tortured in
Egypt at our behest, or languishing for years in
Guantanamo. If we ever release him, we are told, there is a
good chance that he'll go back to terrorism. No kidding!
With no job and his life in tatters, I think he might very
well "go back" whether he has ever been there or not. And

if we don't release him, don't relax. He has a nation of compatriots and friends who will hate us as much as he does.

Whatever else we have to say about torture, regarding the effectiveness or morality or "necessity" of what we all agree is a repugnant practice, it is counterproductive. Any scrap of information gained is swamped by the number and caliber of enemies created. And please don't tell me that it's happening in other countries and not on our own soil so that's okay. It just means we're getting other people to do our dirty work and for no good reason. Again to quote an example, Aywan Zawahri was tortured by the Mubarek regime in the 1980s. Whatever he was before, he is now second in command of Al Qaeda.

The whole argument becomes a tautology. Whether torture works or not, it does not work. The same goes for incarceration without trial. To name just one prominent figure in the above mentioned debate, Professor Alan Dershowitz gives a dozen reasons why the rules of war have to be changed. One is the technical point that we cannot prosecute foreign nationals for crimes not committed on our soil. It is out of our jurisdiction, so we can't do that. Well now, there's a law that could be changed. Change that and send them to Guantanamo after a fair trial. Or if they just happened to be in the wrong place at the wrong time (like me) send them home.

That way you'll have people who cuss you for a while in the unfortunate circumstances. But in the long run, you might even make a friend instead of a permanent enemy.

(*) *Torture and Democracy*, by Darius Rejali, Princeton University Press.

III

ON BEING A VICTIM

The prospect of being arrested in the night and thrown into a cell and threatened with being shot or worse is not something that preoccupies most people. But since it happened to me I have a couple of thoughts on the subject.

To begin with, your captors don't know how they would behave in your situation. They have seen how others behave, but even the toughest of them can't be sure how they would react themselves. They are watching you with interest. Not only for signs of mental or physical weakness, but with a kind of vicarious interest, I believe. The treatment you receive will depend to some extent on what they see.

I don't think you would be tempted to show bravado or defiance in the situation. That would not go down well. But nor does a display of fear. For your own sake if for no other reason you have to hold your head up.

We have all heard those who equate courage with stupidity. As though the only way you'll ever risk your neck is if you're too dim to realize you're doing it. But I think we all know that it's not the weak-minded person we would want beside us in an emergency. Nor is he the one who will be strong in adversity.

The American woman Lori Berenson was pulled off a bus in Peru in 1995 and accused (rightly) of working for an anti-government organization called the Tupac Amaru Revolutionary Movement, the MRTA. After a time of being held in bleak cells with women who had been shot by the police, she was taken to a room in the anti-terrorist headquarters in Lima to meet a group of journalists. Sleep-deprived and angry her hackles were well and truly up.

Berenson took the stage and cursed them out in Spanish. Fists clenched and bellowing she denounced the injustice and suffering in Peru. "In the MRTA there are no criminal terrorists," she told them. "It is a revolutionary movement!" Fifteen years later, the clip is still shown every time her name is mentioned on Peruvian television. Put this in today's context with MRTA replaced by Al Qaeda. (These details can be found in The Liberation of Lori Berenson, by Jennifer Egan, the New York Times Magazine, March 6, 2011.)

After a trial before hooded military judges (at least she got a trial) Berenson was sentenced to life imprisonment. This was later commuted and at time of writing she is free but still in Peru, under the terms of her parole, with her 15-month-old son, who was born in prison.

Berenson was held as a political prisoner but not mistreated or disrespected in spite of her defiance. Some friends and other people wonder if she would have received a lighter sentence if she had shown some panic and despair instead of taking the offensive at the initial hearing. This may be true, but I don't really think so. Political leaders tend to do what they are going to do. Wolfgang Lotz was as nice as ninepence on TV and still got life. In any case Berenson had no choice. A woman who gave up eating meat at the age of eight because of her sympathy for animals was not going to cower and cringe at the age of twenty-six before people she believed were wrong. I have said that I don't recommend angry or defiant behavior. But given the almost worst possible scenario in which she found herself, I'm sure her life is better today for having held her head up all those years.

I am intrigued by the following detail. After her conviction Berenson was flown to the Yanamayo prison in the mountains of Peru. Guarded by armed soldiers she was then transported in a bus with forty other prisoners. Questioned about this, she told the interviewer that she did not remember it as being particularly scary. "You're put in this bus, you can't really hold on because you're handcuffed behind your back, and you need to hold on because you might fall on your face." Smiling at the oddness of it she said, "And so that was your concern."

I remember being pushed along the corridors. I was worried about bumping into things, not about being strapped in a chair and tortured. They were human beings after all. They weren't going to do that. Not to me.

191

Every so often I saw images. My instinct was to try and shove them from my mind. So what are my words of wisdom if God forbid you ever find yourself in the situation?

Above all, don't lose hope. Your manner determines what your captors think of you, which is not unrelated to what comes your way. Don't ask them what has happened to your life. Your guards are acting under orders. They've heard all that before and they don't know the answer anyway. If things get rough, smile your way through it. If someone tries to make you cringe, don't do it. And if there's the threat of torture, ignore it.

If worse comes to worst, I don't suppose there's much meaningful advice that can be given. In waking dreams I've imagined screaming silently to try and drown the pain. I have no idea whether that might work a little bit. The torturer might get me to say this or that (within limits) but he isn't going to win.

And even if he does, he loses.

IV

THE CAPTURE OF BIN LADEN

May, 2011

On Sunday, May 1st of this year a team of Navy Seals raided a home outside Islamabad and killed four people. They were Osama bin Laden, one of his sons, a courier who shot at the invading team, and the courier's wife. When I heard of this my first reaction was relief. A restrained and therefore risky operation had been first ordered and then successfully carried out with a minimum of casualties. There was relief, too, that a chapter in the bin Laden era— and hopefully in the age of international terrorism—had been successfully closed, but that was almost secondary.

In the United States we grant the president enormous power and then essentially tell him what to do. Specifically, the most powerful man on earth soon finds himself surrounded by entrenched groups who will oppose any decision that doesn't suit them. A candidate makes campaign promises which are probably sincere and which he gets to keep if it suits the establishment, not unless. A president like Jimmy Carter who attempts to resist this process will soon pay the price.

In the case of high-priority intelligence like the location of Osama bin Laden, however, there is likely to be enough difference of opinion that it really matters who is the commander in chief. In this case, as in the past, there were two schools of thought – a precision raid or all-out attack. The latter can involve B-2 bombers and fighter jets as well as helicopter gunships and results in mass slaughter in the hope of targeting the enemy. In such cases all evidence is typically destroyed whether the intelligence was accurate or not. But after Sunday, May 1st we *know* the intelligence was accurate and we *know* the raid was successful and the complaints come from – not the local people whose families were *not* destroyed – but from their pride-injured leaders who have been taking our money for decades and using it for their own purposes.

That is Number One. An iconic enemy is dead in an operation that enhances our image in the world instead of further damaging it. Whether or not you are one of those people in the world who believes that United States policies led to 9/11, no one can blame a country for hunting down and killing a national enemy like bin Laden. The fact that he was killed and not taken alive should be no surprise to anyone. I can think of no administration that would relish the unpredictable Pandora's Box of a live bin Laden, saying whatever he would say.

Now it comes to what other people are saying.

Because of the nature of the raid, very few people doubt that bin Laden was in the building and was killed. Neither pictures nor other evidence is necessary – the truth stands out. Discussion about whether local people should have known is specious in my opinion. He could have been three houses down from where I live in New Jersey and I would not have known. Whether intelligence leaders and others should have known is another matter but equally not worth discussing. Divided loyalty and lack of trust is endemic in the region.

The news had hardly broken on that Sunday when the airwaves were filled with many voices taking credit. Torture supporters from the previous administration and their media backers lost no time in telling us how right they were to implement "enhanced interrogations". After ten years of failure during the biggest manhunt in history, their policies had finally paid off.

One of the things I've learned in a traveling life is that if you want to know what's going on in the world these days, you have to think, not just listen. It is not enough to tune into a television channel that supports your political persuasion and believe the first thing you hear. You have to look around, listen, read, and try to find the truth in the words of people who don't always tell it. When I was young we believed that what we read in the national newspapers and heard on the BBC was the plain truth. Rightly or wrongly, we took that as a basis for discussion. In today's world, you cannot do that. Even facts are presented with the spin of power groups. You have to read, listen, think, and sift. You then use what will bring you closer to the truth than the confident words of any number of experts and insiders – your common sense.

Hearing the instant claims for the success of what we call enhanced interrogation, I immediately doubted it. Maybe that shows my predisposition, but one lives and learns. The next day, May 2nd, I saw a brief statement in a national newspaper that was later repeated in a couple of television interviews and led to further reading (*). The statement was that the 9/11 mastermind, Khalid Shaik Mohammed, who was waterboarded literally hundreds of times and subjected to other harsh methods (**) did not betray the trusted courier who was later killed in the bin Laden raid. On the contrary, he denied knowledge of the man, which the interrogators knew to be false, and which therefore focused their attention on the courier. When I saw that I recognized the truth. It was not coercion that worked in the end. It was intelligent interrogation and analysis.

Obviously, I can be accused of doing just what so many of us do on a regular basis – seeing what fits my preconceived ideas and accepting it. I can't prove otherwise. But in response to this momentous news event, I have one more comment on the subject of interrogation.

Many people feel that if we tell the world that we are never going to use torture, the captured terrorists will just laugh at us. Well, I was arrested and not tortured and I doubt they would be laughing: but that could be debated – there was after all the threat of torture. What scared me even more was the thought of being tried and found guilty like Wolfgang Lotz or Lori Berenson. Our current policy is to hold people without trial and use "enhanced interrogation". In spite of campaign promises, our current president has been persuaded to go along with that. Maybe there are practical considerations. But I know from experience that people who want something can always tell you why they want it. And as already argued, I doubt the value of coercion – even serious coercion. What then?

Pressed to the wall on it, I am not saying that we should tell the world that we'll never use rough tactics. I would not go on the Internet and put up signs saying, "This is a No Torture Zone." Let the captured person worry about that and what he's heard and what is going to happen in his case. But I wish we could have trials. And I certainly want my country to treat even our worst enemies as human beings, however much we despise their activities.

As a last word let me quote a kind of parable. A lawyer who defended revolutionaries in Peru, Anibal Apari from Lima, who is the father of Lori Berenson's son, was a member of the openly Marxist but initially moderate MRTA. The group was started in the early 1980s in opposition not only to the government but to the more violent Shining Path, a revolutionary terrorist group in Peru which has been compared to the Khmer Rouge. At its inception, according to Apari, the MRTA stressed that the essence of successful armed struggle is to *respect your enemy*. These may sound like strange words in the age of international terrorism, and I know the situation is very different. But the philosophy worked well in El Salvador, Brazil, Uruguay, Nicaragua, and Cuba, where the current presidents are all former guerrillas. A similar approach, without the use of violence, is identified with Martin Luther King in the United States. The MRTA failed in Peru, according to Apari, because it gave in to extremist elements (like al Qaeda) and lost respect all around.

(*) *Behind The Hunt For Bin Laden*, by Mark Mazzetti, Helene Cooper and Peter Baker, NY Times, May 2nd 2011. (**) *Harsh Methods of Questioning Debated Again*, by Scott Shane and Charlie Savage, NY Times, May 4, 2011)

V

AFTERWORD

When Tom Clancy was publishing *Red Storm Rising,* which, like *The Hunt for Red October,* he had written after attending the non-classified talks at many Defense Department conferences, he was informed by government officials that some of what he had written was highly sensitive information. Clancy immediately said, "Tell me what it is and it's out of there." The response was, "We can't do that, you dummy, it's classified!"

In writing this memoir I have made free use of what I know firsthand of what happened in Cairo in 1965. I have also reported some of what we discussed at the time in the spirit of educated conjecture, and I know how this can relate to facts that are not made public. Not being privy to what might be classified, I have used real names where I recall them, except for some that I have chosen to withhold. If this or any other material is considered sensitive in any quarter, I can only apologize and repeat that my intention is simply to tell the story as I recall it.

Norman Lang
July, 2011

Made in the USA
Charleston, SC
20 September 2011